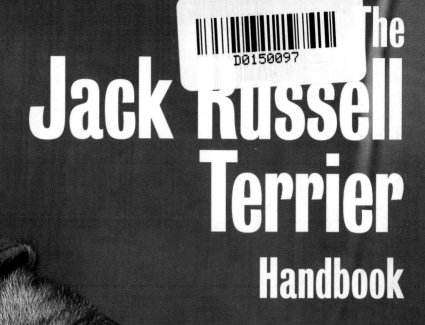

# The Jack Russell Terrier

## Handbook

D. Caroline Coile, Ph.D.

**With Full-color Photos and Drawings by Michele Earle-Bridges**

BARRON'S

## About the Author

D. Caroline Coile is an award-winning author who has written 16 books and over 100 articles about dogs for both scientific and lay publications. She holds a Ph.D. in the field of neuroscience and behavior, with special interests in canine sensory systems, genetics, and behavior. Her dogs have been nationally ranked in conformation, obedience, and field-trial competition.

## Acknowledgments

The information contained in this book comes from a variety of sources: breeders, original research, scientific articles, and veterinary journals. But by far my most heartfelt gratitude must go to my most demanding teachers, who have taught me the skills of both home repair and dog repair, and whetted my curiosity (and carpets) about everything canine for the past 30 years: Baha, Khyber, Tundra, Kara, Hypatia, Savannah, Sissy, Dixie, Bobby, Kitty, Jeepers, Beanie, Junior, Khyzi, Wolfman, Stinky, Omen, Isis, Minka, Honey, and Luna.

Breed standards are reprinted courtesy of the JRTAA, JRTCA, and AKC.

*All inquiries should be addressed to:*
Barron's Educational Series, Inc.
250 Wireless Boulevard
Hauppauge, New York 11788
http://www.barronseduc.com

International Standard Book No. 0-7641-1411-5

*Library of Congress Catalog Card No. 00-022523*

## Library of Congress Cataloging-in-Publication Data

Coile, D. Caroline.
    The Jack Russell terrier handbook / D. Caroline Coile.
        p.    cm.
    Includes bibliographical references (p.    ).
    ISBN 0-7641-1411-5 (alk. pbk.)
    1. Jack Russell terrier. I. Title.
SF429.J27 C64    2000
636.755—dc21                                    00-022523

Printed in Hong Kong

9 8 7 6 5 4 3

## Photo Credits

Isabelle Francais: pages vi, 7, 14, 21, 22, 24, 28 left, 28 right, 43, 45, 52, 58, 62, 67, 70, 77, 82, 88, 90, 95, 108, 110, 118, 120, 134, 143, 158, 160, 168, 176, 183, 186; Norvia Behling: pages vii, 5, 17, 30, 36, 38, 40, 47, 50, 75, 84, 94, 136, 141, 147, 150, 152, 159, 170, 179, 190; Judith Strom: pages viii, 60, 73, 113, 115, 128, 148, 195; Sharon Eide: pages 2, 4, 96, 130; Kent and Donna Dannen: pages 9, 81, 103, 105, 125; Elizabeth Flynn: pages 10, 33, 35, 86, 92, 132, 165, 180; Bonnie Nance: pages 18, 55, 74, 111, 184; Tara Darling: pages 56, 100, 127; Joan Balzarini: pages 65, 80, 98; Paulette Braun: page 68; Dale Jackson: page 101; Mella Panzella: page 163.

## Cover Photos

Isabelle Francais.

**Important Note**

This pet handbook tells the reader how to buy or adopt, and care for a Jack Russell Terrier. The author and the publisher consider it important to point out that the advice given in the book is meant primarily for normally developed dogs of excellent physical health and good character.

Anyone who adopts a fully grown dog should be aware that the animal has already formed its basic impressions of human beings. The new owner should watch the animal carefully, including its behavior toward humans, and should meet the previous owner.

If the dog comes from a shelter, it may be possible to get some information on the dog's background and peculiarities there. There are dogs that, as a result of bad experiences with humans, behave in an unnatural manner or may even bite. Only people that have experience with dogs should take in such animals.

Caution is further advised in the association of children with dogs, in meeting with other dogs, and in exercising the dog without a leash.

Even well-behaved and carefully supervised dogs sometimes do damage to someone else's property or cause accidents. It is therefore in the owner's interest to be adequately insured against such eventualities, and we strongly urge all dog owners to purchase a liability policy that covers their dog.

# Contents

# Preface

Jack Russell Terriers are not your run of the mill dog. They live life to its fullest, and if you're lucky, they'll let you join in the fun. They can pack more adventures into one day than most other dogs can do in a month. They require people who are more prepared to cope with the many surprises that life with a Jack Russell will surely serve up, and their people need more information than the average dog owner.

*The Jack Russell Terrier Handbook* was written for the Jack owner who needs a little more advanced information about living with a Jack. This book assumes some basic knowledge about dog care; if you need beginner information you are urged to consult my introductory book, *Jack Russell Terriers: A Complete Pet Owner's Manual.* This book was written to prepare the owner who wants to excel at Jack Russell ownership. Jack Russell Terriers have so much to offer, and you have so much to give, but you may both need a little guidance. Your Jack will keep you on your toes, so be ready!

*Ahhh—the good life!*

## Chapter One

# The Jack From Way Back

It's very dark. Her body fits so snugly against the sides of the tunnel that any light from the entrance is blocked. Yet she presses on. Here the space narrows and she must push with all her might to pass; here she must dig to widen the passage; here she must push aside an obstacle in her path. She will not let anything deter her. This labyrinth beneath the surface is her only world now, to follow this scent that draws her deeper and deeper her only purpose. Perhaps she is part of a hunt preparing to bolt a holed fox; perhaps she is in a barn in pursuit of a fleeing rodent; perhaps she is at a terrier trial facing a caged rat; or perhaps she is under the bed sheets hot on the trail of some imaginary dastardly vermin. She is a Jack Russell Terrier, and this is the world to which she was born and to which she is inevitably drawn.

# Terrier Roots Are in the Earth

At least as long ago as 200 B.C. small dogs called *agassoei* were

*A breed forged for the hunt . . .*

being used to follow wild animals underground. Skeletal evidence of a dog with terrier-like dimensions has been found in Europe from shortly after that time period. The Romans dubbed these dogs that worked in the earth *terrarii*, from the Latin *terra,* for earth. By the sixteenth century treatises on dogs mentioned terriers (or "terrars") and how to hunt with them.

## Ancient History

An early description of terriers reads: "Another sorte which hunteth the Foxe and the Badger or Grey onely, whom we call Terrars, because they (after the manner and custom of Ferrets in searching for Connyes) creepe into the grounde, and by that means make afrayde, nyppe, and byte the Fox and the badger in such sort, that eyther they teare them in peeces with thayre teeth beying in the bosome of the earth, or else hayle and pull them perforce out of their lurking angles, dark dongeons and close caves…"—Johannes Caius, in his *De Canibus Anglicis,* 1576.

Terriers have never received the illustrious attention showered on

*Today's JRT is little changed from those that proved themselves in the early fox hunts.*

dogs more often associated with nobility through the centuries, but they have been there all along, helping to rid farms and homes of vermin, and in the process, providing some sport for the commoner. Not until their use was recognized as vital for aiding in otter hunting with hounds did they come to the attention of the upper classes. Already adept at bolting foxes, the terriers were a natural choice to join the newly emerging sport of fox hunting.

## The Fox Hunt

Fox hunting gained interest in the eighteenth century, and throughout the next century evolved into a more formal, faster-paced event that gained great favor with the gentry. Although some hunts had their terriers run with the hounds, many could not keep up, and they were often so tired when they arrived at the hole they were not in the best form to face a fox. Instead the terriers often were carried by a rider in a type of saddle bag, and then released fresh at the hole. Before a hunt, as many foxholes as possible would be barricaded to prevent the fox from immediately holing up, but the fox would often find other holes, bringing the hunt to a stop. The terriers would then be sent down the hole while the hounds were held back. In short order barking could be heard from below ground, as the terrier confronted the fox. A terrier that was too soft to face the fox was unsuited for the task, as was a terrier so aggressive that it attacked and killed the fox.

If the hunters were fortunate, the terrier would convince the fox that it was better off facing the pack above ground than the terrier below, and the fox would bolt and the hunt would continue. Some concern was given for the times the terrier would also bolt from the hole in chase, as the hounds could mistake it for the fox in their excitement and jump upon it. For this reason white terriers were often preferred, because the hounds would be less likely to mistake a white dog for a fox. The terrier man would remain behind to collect the terrier, the unsung hero of the hunt. Sometimes the fox could not be persuaded to bolt; in such cases the hunt would eventually go off in search of another and the terrier man would be left to dig out his tenacious terrier, who would continue to harass the fox until pulled from the hole. Then, perhaps with a few cuts and bruises to show for her efforts, the terrier would try to rejoin the hunt, ready for the next recalcitrant fox.

## The Perfect Terrier

As the English became increasingly enchanted with the sport of fox hunting, larger hunts emerged that included many hounds and terriers. This surge in popularity allowed for special attention to be paid to perfecting the terriers on whom the success of the hunt depended so greatly. Different strains evolved in different areas, including the Old English Black and Tan as well as the predominantly white Fox Terrier.

Terriers were a working dog, bred to do a job. Purity of breeding and smartness of appearance were of

---

## TERRIER-IFIC!

### Trump

Trump was described as follows: "In the first place the colour is white, with just a patch of dark tan over each eye and ear; whilst a similar dot, not larger than a penny piece, marks the root of the tail. The coat, which is thick, close, and trifle wiry, is calculated to protect the body from wet and cold, but has no affinity with the long rough jacket of the Scotch Terrier. The legs are straight as arrows, the feet perfect. The loins and conformation of the whole frame indicative of the hardihood and endurance, while the height of the animal may be compared to that of a full-grown vixen fox."

*The 1800s witnessed the emergence of a new breed of terrier.*

With the coming of the industrial age, many former rural people, who had always enjoyed animal sports as a way of life, devised new animal sports suited to an urban lifestyle. They quickly found that the terrier's rat killing ability could be easily transformed into a betting and entertainment spectacle. Contests centered on how long it took a terrier to kill sometimes hundreds of rats within a small enclosure. Unlike the traditional fox hunting terrier, which was expected to harass but not kill, a successful rat pit terrier had to kill quickly. Crosses with bull breeds were made to produce a dog that was more likely to kill instantly. Such dogs were great in the rat pits, but poor in the fox burrows, as they tended to attack the fox; what was worse, they did so without uttering a sound to inform the hunter of their location underground. Crosses to Beagles not only helped improve scenting ability, but tempered the tendency to attack, and brought back the tendency to bark. These breeds, along with other terriers, have all probably been introduced into the dogs that eventually became the Jack Russell Terrier; nonetheless, the JRT retains its own identity that is true to the Parson's original Fox Terriers.

Different terrains and hunting preferences favored slightly different terrier attributes, and terrier men seldom agreed on what made a perfect fox hunting terrier. This, coupled with the difficulty of transporting dogs over great distances for breed-

comparatively little importance. It was not uncommon to experiment by crossing a terrier with a dog of another breed, or even another mix, in order to create a better working dog. Crosses with Bulldogs for courage, Beagles for scenting prowess, and even Greyhounds for speed all were incorporated in the quest for the perfect fox hunting terrier. The influence of terriers bred mainly for rat killing ability can still be seen in some terriers bred mainly for fox hunting.

ing, led to the existence of a wide variety of types associated with different regions and hunts. Among these Fox Terriers were some very able, predominantly white bodied, dogs. By the middle 1800s, strains from the Midland packs such as the Rufford, the Oakley, the Grove, the Belvoir, and the Quorn, were already established and respected.

# The Sporting Parson

Although keeping a pack of fox hounds was an expensive undertaking, keeping the terriers for the pack was not. A man of more modest means could partake in all the excitement and splendor of a hunt if he could be designated the terrier man of the hunt. The same terriers could also provide good sport with a single hunter, another plus for a hunter more concerned with the sport than the pageantry. Such a man was the Parson John Russell.

Born in 1795, John Russell developed an early passion for hunting. While away at boarding school he and a friend illicitly kept a small pack of hounds in a local blacksmith's care and hunted with them at every opportunity—an escapade that nearly got him expelled. Despite his diversions, Russell gained entrance to Exeter College at Oxford University, the locale and freedom of which afforded him access to more hunting. Although his finances would not

allow him a pack of his own, he learned from some of the top huntsmen of the day, gaining knowledge that he valued at least as much as that he was learning in his classes. The experience allowed him to appreciate the fine terriers used in the hunt, and to get an impression of what he would consider the ideal fox hunting terrier.

*The JRT was bred to keep up with horses galloping on the hunt.*

5

## Parson Russell's Terrier

The story goes that one day in 1819, while walking in town, Russell happened upon a milkman with a terrier that epitomized his ideal. Some speculation exists that this was, in fact, not a chance meeting and that Russell had previously arranged to see the dog (the milkman being known for breeding good terriers). Whatever the circumstance, the dog met his every expectation and he bought her on the spot. Although her background and her subsequent matings, if they were ever publicly known, have been lost, "Trump" was to become the foundation of Russell's distinctive line of Fox Terriers.

The following year, Russell was ordained and moved near South Moulton, where he assembled an odd pack of hounds and hunted otter at every chance. He also struck up a friendship with a learned huntsman, George Templar, whose foxhounds eventually formed the core of Russell's pack upon Templar's death. After marrying in 1826, Russell moved to Iddesleigh, where he had even greater opportunity to hunt. Still on a limited budget, he merged his pack with that of a wealthier neighbor, and soon their dogs gained a reputation as talented fox hunters—although their hunts still lacked the trappings of the more prestigious hunts. The Parson became well known as "The Sporting Parson," and hunted at every chance almost until his death at the age of 88.

# The Dog Show

One of the most defining events in the history of purebred dogs occurred with the advent of the first dog show in 1859. The first classes for Fox Terriers were offered in 1863. Although many theories had previously existed concerning the relationship of form and function, such evaluations had always been tested in the field by the dog's performance. With conformation shows, adherence to the standard was the endpoint, with no performance test necessary to defend the judge's choice. Yet many of the most essential characteristics of a working terrier cannot be fully evaluated in the confines of a dog show ring. In addition, competition based upon certain physical traits tends to lead to exaggeration of those traits. Dog shows became incredibly popular, however, and one of the stars of the show was the clever-looking Fox Terrier.

The Parson Russell entered his Fox Terriers at one of the first shows

*TERRIER-IFIC!*

The first Parson Jack Russell English Champion was Winnie the Witch of Hardytown; the first male Champion was Cassacre Boatswain; the first Championship show group winner was Mindlen Hoolet of Muhlross; and the first Junior warrant winner was Mindlen Hairy Minnow.

in which they could be shown, but he lost interest in showing them and subsequently limited his dog show participation to judging. His reputation as a respected hound and terrier authority was immense, and he was one of the original founders of the Kennel Club in England, even judging at their first sanctioned show in 1874. Even by that time Fox Terriers had begun to take on a new, showier look. Compared to them, John Russell's Fox Terriers tended to be smaller, with far more white, and less coat, than most of the others. Despite the fact that he declined to show his own dogs, many of the show Fox Terriers could trace back to his stock. And in fact, many modern Fox Terriers descend in part from the Parson's dogs. However, they were changed dramatically from the Parson's image of what the Fox Terrier should be. As Fox Terrier show devotees centered their attention on the ring, rather than the field, they created the most extraordinary show dog of the day, but it was no longer the dog of choice for the hunt. That honor remained with John Russell's terriers.

## Dirty Work

After John Russell's death in 1883, Arthur Heinemann, who had collected many descendents of Russell's dogs, became the breed's guardian and major proponent. In 1894, Heinemann, along with other working Fox Terrier enthusiasts, formed what was to become the Par-

*Jacks are as interested in what goes on underground as above.*

son Jack Russell Terrier Club, with the purpose to "promote the breeding of the old-fashioned North Devon type of Fox Terrier, as bred and made famous by Rev. J. Russell." Badger digging had become very popular at the time, and the new club was quick to sponsor badger digs as a means of testing their terriers away from the fox hunt.

A badger dig often attracted a large crowd, who brought picnic lunches and settled in for a day's entertainment. Several terriers would be taken to a badger's labyrinth of tunnels that made up its sett, and one would be sent in. The terrier would get to the badger, holding it at bay while the people dug toward the sound of the ruckus. After several hours the terrier might emerge, to be replaced with a fresh terrier, while digging resumed. This was usually an all day affair, climaxed by the terriers dragging out the badger. The badger was not to be killed, but rather caught, bagged, weighed, and released.

By 1900, the differences in the new show type Fox Terriers and the old working type were so blatant that a few shows offered classes for both types. In 1904 Heinemann wrote the

first breed standard, which still survives as the basis for current standards. The separate classes never caught on; those interested in showing preferred the showier Fox Terrier, whereas those with the old working type either feared that showing them would send them along the same path as the show Fox Terrier, or simply were more interested in working them in the field. The Fox Terrier had been inevitably split into a new, show version and an old, working version. By World War I the new Fox Terrier had become the darling of England, extraordinarily popular not only as a show dog but as a pet. Its working relation kept a lower profile, finding favor with sportsmen and farmers who appreciated its talents.

# The Lost Years

Arthur Heinemann died in 1930, and his terriers, the only remaining dogs that could boast of being at least predominantly descended from the Parson's dogs, were dispersed. In fact, many people contend that these were the last dogs that could genuinely lay claim to being real Jack Russell Terriers. The Parson had sold many pups during his lifetime, however, and their descendents could be found with hunters around the region. Many of these hunters were not concerned with keeping the lines pure, and in true working terrier tradition the dogs had sometimes been crossed with other good working terriers.

## The Real Jack Russell?

Because the Jack Russell Terrier was not recognized by the Kennel Club, many small, predominantly white, terrier mixes assumed the identities of Jack Russell Terriers. These dogs became popular as family pets after World War II. In addition, dogs that had been purposefully bred with shorter legs gained favor with the public. Soon these dogs were the ones generally referred to as Jack Russell Terriers. The ensuing years were filled with crossbreeding and with misunderstandings about whether a Jack Russell Terrier was a true breed rather than any small, white terrier of dubious ancestry. Additionally, public acceptance of a short-legged version in preference to the original longer legged terrier as the real JRT, threatened the original Jack Russell Terrier's future.

In the 1970s, several clubs, including the Jack Russell Terrier Club of Great Britain (JRTCGB) and the South East Jack Russell Terrier Club (SEJRTC) were formed to promote the JRT. The JRTCGB opted to recognize a large range of sizes (10 to 15 inches [25–37 cm]) as correct for the breed, whereas the SEJRTC set a height limit of 13 inches (32 cm), promoting only the smaller and often shorter legged Jacks. The JRTCGB was opposed to Kennel Club recognition for any Jack Russell Terrier, fearing it would spell the demise of the working terrier. In contrast, the SEJRTC worked to have their standard recognized by the Kennel Club. This alarmed proponents of the

*With a long history of equine association, the JRT is a familiar sight around the stables.*

*T E R R I E R - I F I C !*

The most well-known JRT in the world is probably the captivating "Wishbone," star of his own Emmy winning television series. Wishbone, whose real name is Willowall Soccer, beat out over 100 other dogs vying for the role. His fame is closely contested by Moose, better known as "Eddie," on the television series *Frasier*.

traditional longer legged JRT, who saw Kennel Club recognition of the short-legged terriers as Jack Russell Terriers as the possible death blow to the long-legged dogs.

Since the JRTCB would not act to promote recognition of the long-legged Jacks, in 1983 other traditional JRT enthusiasts resurrected the dormant Parson Jack Russell Terrier Club of Great Britain (PJRTCGB) in order to gain Kennel Club recognition for the long-legged terriers. The ensuing arguments and confusion caused the Kennel Club to reject the applications for recognition by both the SEJRT and the PJRTCGB, although persistent efforts finally brought about recognition of the PJRTCGB standard, and the newly dubbed Parson Jack Russell Terrier in 1990.

# American Jacks

Although the history of the breed in America was quite different from that in England, by the 1970s a similar situation of lost breed identity existed. Terriers had always been far less important in American fox hunting, and many hunts did not even include a terrier. The Fox Terrier had traditionally been mainly a pet and show dog in North America; working

*The short-legged (or English) Jack Russell Terrier is specialized for close work in tight spaces.*

terriers were used mostly for ratting and other vermin hunting on foot. Thus, the traditional long-legged JRT never gained a strong foothold in America. The shorter legged type of JRT became a fixture around farms, stables, and homes, however.

## The Jack Russell Terrier Club of America

In 1976 the Jack Russell Terrier Club of America (JRTCA) was formed, adopting the Heinemann standard favoring the taller, traditional JRT known as the Parson Jack Russell Terrier in Britain. In fact, the JRTCA owns the trademark to the name "Parson Jack Russell Terrier" in the United States, a situation that prevented another club from adopting that name. From its inception, the JRTCA was adamantly opposed to American Kennel Club (AKC) or any all-breed registry recognition. It sought to promote the JRT as a working terrier rather than a pure breed, and the JRTCA registered dogs based upon a more stringent set of criteria than did the purely pedigree based AKC.

## The Jack Russell Terrier Breeder's Association

Not all JRT fanciers agreed that the JRTCA mandate against AKC recognition was in the best interests of the breed. They formed the Jack Russell Terrier Breeder's Association (JRTBA) in 1985 to promote the traditional Parson type Jack Russell Terrier through AKC recognition. As this goal was the very antithesis of the

JRTCA's vision of what was best for the breed, a heated and acrimonious battle ensued. Despite widespread

---

### ✫ JACK FACT ✫

**Going Underground**

Most terriers in North America never have the opportunity to go to ground after real quarry. The difficulty in finding appropriate quarry, coupled with safety concerns, makes it hard for most terrier owners to work their dogs in the field. And aside from the intrinsic value of the outing, there was little to be gained in terms of recognition from such endeavors. In 1971, the American Working Terrier Association (AWTA) formed, which offered terriers the chance to prove their mettle underground in a safe circumstance, and also recognized those dogs that demonstrated their working talents. When the JRTCA formed in 1976, they adopted the basic ideas of the AWTA den trials to establish their own go-to-ground trials, as well as to recognize dogs that demonstrated their abilities as actual hunting terriers in the field. The AKC followed suit by establishing earthdog trials in 1994. These terrier trials, while not perfect, once again allow terriers to test their instincts, and their owners to appreciate what these dogs were bred to do. See pages 127–130 for more information.

opposition within the breed, the AKC granted recognition to the Jack Russell Terrier, with the breed admitted as a regular member of the Terrier group in the year 2000.

## Recognition Rift

The rift between the JRTCA and the JRTBA, now renamed the Jack Russell Terrier Association of America (JRTAA) remains deep. So adamant is the JRTCA against the breed's participation in AKC events that owners who compete in them are barred from competition in JRTCA events. This rule forces Jack Russell owners to decide between the two registries, a situation that only serves to further divide and harm the breed.

The JRTCA is not acting out of pettiness. They are instead acting out of loyalty to the ideals of the Parson John Russell, who recognized very soon after the advent of dog shows their deleterious effect upon working qualities. Beyond that, they have witnessed firsthand the damage done to breeds by disreputable breeders cashing in on the selling value of the letters *AKC* in a puppy ad.

## Current Dangers

Yet the Jack Russell Terrier may face a far greater danger from an exploding popularity based in part on its media image and irresistible nature. Media stars portraying the breed at its impish best have made the JRT more visible than ever before in its history. They have won many friends for the breed and brought many families to the dog of their dreams. Yet too many people want a Jack Russell Terrier without realizing the dog they want is really a working terrier with hunting on its mind. The JRTCA and the JRTAA are finding themselves united in the common cause of educating prospective owners and rescuing dogs abandoned by those they failed to reach in time.

Today most Jack Russell Terriers live as family pets. They have redirected their hunting talents to searching out grasshoppers, chasing balls, excavating gardens, and leading their families on merry chases. Some compete in dog shows, terrier races, or earthdog, agility, tracking, or obedience trials. Some continue to hunt. Still the acknowledged master of the hunt, the Jack Russell Terrier has once again proven it can catch whatever it sets its sights on—including the hearts of families around the world.

# Short-legged Jack Russell Terriers

In the United States, the long-legged dogs have been recognized by the JRTCA and the AKC as the real Jack Russell Terrier. Some long-legged fanciers consider the short-legged Jacks as virtual imposters to the Jack Russell name, and refuse to acknowledge them as Jack Russell Terriers. Those who live with and love the shorter legged Jacks (often called "Shorties" or "Puddin's") would disagree.

## When Short Legs Are Better Than Long

The shorter Jacks never pretended to be show dogs, nor were they ever bred with show characteristics in mind. Instead they were bred to do a job—a somewhat different job than the long-legged Jacks. The shorter legged Jack was perfect for hunting on foot. These little dogs were unrivaled as all-around hunters and exterminators of vermin in the field and around the farm. The latter talent made them popular at horse stables, where they not only controlled rats but caught the attention of riders and grooms, who often took a cute Puddin' pup into their homes. The Puddin' Jack became the unofficial mascot of the English horse set, proving itself to be a lively companion around the stables and home. Non-horsy friends who met the irresistible scamps adopted one for their own pet, and the Puddin' Jack took over as the popular image of the Jack Russell Terrier.

## The Great Leg Controversy

As the Puddin's displaced the longer legged Jacks, proponents of traditional Jacks justifiably worried that their breed's identity was being lost. They argued that these Puddin's weren't really Jack Russell Terriers, but almost certainly resulted from crosses with shorter legged terriers. But Puddin' breeders countered that the longer legged Jacks, while more like the Parson's, also could not trace their lineage back to the Parson's dogs with confidence and possibly carried just as much foreign blood.

The JRTCA set a height limit that excluded the shortest of the short-legged Jacks, relegating them to nonregistered status and barring them from competitions. The JRTBA standard also excluded the short-legged dogs, and when the AKC accepted this standard as the official standard of the newly recognized Jack Russell Terrier, the Puddin' seemed destined to be a dog without a breed. Yet it remained by far the more popular of the two types, and every bit as worthy of recognition in the eyes of its many admirers. Rather than continue the unrewarding fight to have their dogs included as Jack Russell Terriers, enthusiasts have instead elected to embrace the little Jack's own history and promote it as a separate breed.

## A New Name

Because of its hunting ability and its identification with the hunt, the Puddin' had often been called the Hunt Terrier. It was felt, however, that this name might elicit opposition given the antihunting sentiment in many circles. Instead, the name English Jack Russell Terrier was adopted as a fitting description of this breed's heritage. In 1996 the English Rustler's Terrier Club was formed to promote the short-legged terriers as a separate entity, followed by the English Jack Russell Terrier Club of America. These clubs were replaced by the English Jack Russell Terrier Club Alliance (EJRTCA) in 1999.

## Chapter Two
# Hit the Jackpot!

Jack Russell Terriers are cute, loving, and lots of fun—so irresistible it's hard not to bring home the first one you can. But every bit of fun of owning any dog is mirrored by an equal dose of work and worry—and Jack Russell Terriers are lots and lots of fun. Taking care of a Jack takes time, energy, money, and commitment. For that investment, you will get back very few tangible rewards. Luckily, it is the intangible reward that proves that you *can* buy love… just make sure you get the best love money can buy.

## You Don't Know Jack!

If you think that all Jack Russell Terriers are smart and obedient like the ones on television you are only half right. They are smart—very smart. But obedient? Never!

### Is a Jack Russell Right for You?

The Jack Russell Terrier is the ideal dog for a person with a sense of adventure, an even bigger sense

*Have you met your match?*

of humor, and unlimited patience. Generations of selection for working ability has produced the perfect hunting terrier, a dog that must be bold, energetic, inquisitive, and relentless. The working terrier must rely on its own choices and instincts when deep underground; no person is there to make decisions. This means they must be independent and self-directed (even when their owners give them commands to the contrary). They must be tough and tenacious in the face of adversity (even if that adversity is their owner telling them *No!*). They must be untiring in order to follow the fox over great distances and keep it at bay for long periods (as any owner knows who has ever tried to catch a runaway JRT). They must bark with vigor and stamina (much to the next door neighbor's dismay). They must be able to solve problems on their own (even if that problem is how to break out of the yard). They must be eager to chase quarry (even if it's your beloved cat). They must be anxious to go underground (even if that means getting stuck under the porch and riddling the yard with holes). Allowed to roam the neighborhood,

### Good or Bad?

Jack Russell Terriers are not the ideal dog for all people. Some common JRT traits that make the JRT perfect for some people make it terrible for others.

• Jack Russell Terriers are energetic. That's great if you are a get-up-and-go kind of person who seeks adventure with a canine accomplice. It's not if you are already overwhelmed with work and value what little relaxation time you have left.

• Jack Russell Terriers are hunters. That's great if you enjoy hunting. It's not if you expect your dog to trot nicely by your side at all times, stay in the yard when you leave the gate open, or act kindly toward the neighbor's cat (or even yours!).

• Jack Russell Terriers love to dig and explore. That's great if you have a place for them to do so. It's not if you demand a perfect yard or don't like dirty footprints across your carpet.

• Jack Russell Terriers are feisty. That's great if you don't give them a chance to abuse that feistiness. It's not if you have young children or in some cases, other dogs.

• Jack Russell Terriers are smart. That's great if you want a dog you can train and challenge. It's not great if you can't spend lots of time stimulating its mind every day.

• Jack Russell Terriers are strong-willed. That's great if you want a dog that will stick to task in the face of adversity. It's not if you want a dog that will obey you without question.

---

the JRT feels compelled to range far afield and may not return for days, or at all; in fact, some JRT's have been found ensconced underground after days, unwilling to leave their quarry at any cost. To some, this describes the dog of their dreams; to others, it is a nightmare.

Jack Russell Terriers absolutely must have the chance to exercise both their body and mind with daily outdoor activity; otherwise, they are likely to exercise both by creating special effects in your home with their teeth and nails. Owners who want a JRT primarily as a pet must commit themselves to changing their lifestyles to fit that of the JRT, because compromise is not in this breed's vocabulary!

Although JRT's require an inordinate amount of exercise, they can derive as much joy from killing toys in your living room as they could rats in the field. They will provide their family with hours of entertainment with their impish sense of humor and clownish antics. They learn quickly

*Who says Jacks and cats can't be friends?*

and are eager to please as long as there is some fun involved. JRT's are excellent watchdogs; a few can even be menacing protection dogs. They can make fun-loving friends for children, too, but they will not put up with any abusive treatment. They are not the breed of choice for very young children who may not realize that they are being rough.

## Jacks and Other Pets

Terriers are notorious for quarreling with each other, but JRT's are bred to get along with other members of a hunting pack. However, not all JRT's have this proper outlook. Moreover, many have been crossed with less amiable terriers in the quest for a JRT that could actually kill the fox (a fellow canid), resulting in some JRT's that are not compatible with other dogs. In most families, two JRT's of the opposite sex will get along just fine; however, a third JRT may not fit in so well. It is especially not advisable to leave more than two JRT's alone and unsupervised. If you have more than two JRT's, be warned that other dogs will often jump on and attack the loser in a scuffle. Neutered dogs are less likely to fight, and neutering will prevent the headache of keeping Jack and Jill separated during her seasons. Nor are JRT's good with hamsters, gerbils, ferrets, and cats, unless raised with them or otherwise carefully trained and supervised.

# Looking for Trouble

You've been warned! Once you invite that whirling dervish with the innocent "Who me?" response to all your corrections, your life will never be boring. You'll be on your toes for the next 15 years, chasing, cleaning, repairing, training, laughing, and loving, so now's the time to make sure the dog you're making all these sacrifices for is the best companion you can find. It's not hard to find a Jack Russell Terrier, but if you want one that represents the breed at its finest, you can hedge your bet by choosing your source carefully. To do that, you need to know how to tell good breeders from bad breeders, and good Jacks from great Jacks.

*Jacks can be playful and loving companions for considerate young people.*

## Why Do You Want a Jack Russell?

Everyone wants a good, healthy companion; in addition, some people want a reliable hunting partner or a competitive show dog. Most Jack Russell Terriers can be easily trained to be good hunting terriers. If regular hunting is an important function to you, then you will do best to find a Jack from a line of dogs that is regularly used for hunting or that has earned earthdog titles. Although Jack Russell Terriers have not traditionally been show dogs, some breeders have paid more attention to producing dogs conforming to the standard, and have competed successfully in conformation events. Although other aspects of a good JRT should not be compromised simply for looks, the best of these breeders are producing Jacks that are not only good show specimens, but also competent hunters and healthy companions. Because more than one standard for the breed exists, make sure the line conforms to the standard of the organization in which you plan to compete.

Most people seeking a new JRT don't want a hunting or competition dog, just a new best friend. Their most common sources are newspaper ads, friends, pet stores, hobby breeders, and rescue. Of these, hobby breeders and rescue organizations should be your first choices.

**Hobby breeders:** Hobby breeders have made producing superior Jack Russell Terriers a main focus of their lives. They will have proven their dogs in some form of work or competition and screened them for hereditary health problems. Despite their best efforts, not every pup will turn out to be competition quality. These "pet-quality" pups will still have profited from the breeder's knowledge of genetics and puppy care, and will still need good homes. Good hobby breeders will screen prospective pet homes no less diligently than their other prospective homes, and will expect you to keep them abreast of your pup's progress and come to them with your problems just like all of their puppy buyers.

Hobby breeders can be located through Jack Russell Terrier clubs, dog magazines (especially Jack Russell Terrier magazines), or kennel pages on the Internet. As in all walks of life, some breeders are more ethical and knowledgeable than others. Try to visit prospective breeders personally and see for yourself how the adults look and act, and how puppies are being raised.

A great place to find breeders is at a JRTCA event or an AKC Jack Russell Terrier specialty show (a prestigious show in which only Jack Russell Terriers compete). The annual JRTCA National Trial attracts hundreds of competitors in conformation and performance events. The annual JRTAA National Specialty is the premier AKC event for Jacks in the United States, also attracting the best Jack Russell Terriers from around the country. Not only can you meet more good breeders at large

specialties, but you can also get a better idea of the particular style of Jack you prefer and what traits are most important to you.

# Puppy Picking

Even if you have no competitive goals, remember the essentials of any good Jack: good health, good temperament, and good looks.

## Good Health

For *health*, ask about the longevity and health of your potential pup's ancestors. Don't discount a line with some problems, as no line of dogs is perfect, and besides, some other breeders may simply not be as honest in disclosing problems. JRTCA registered Jacks have passed some veterinary health clearances (such as those certifying normal eyes and patellas) in order to be registered, but these are minimal tests. A veterinary certificate of normal hearing, thyroid function, and lack of allergies or seizures is a definite plus, but it's somewhat unusual to find a litter with all of these health clearances. If you want a male for conformation (or breeding), be sure he has both testicles descended into the scrotum by the time you take him home. They should both be down by eight weeks of age, although some may be as late as 16 weeks (or in very rare cases, longer). No matter how much research you do into the background of any puppy, there is no guarantee that your dog will live a long and healthy life, but you can increase the odds by choosing a dog from a healthy family.

## Good Temperament

For *temperament*, consider the essentials of the Jack Russell Terrier standard. The Jack Russell Terrier should be eager, alert, and self-confident. It's human nature to go for the extremes in temperament, but for most family companions you're better off to choose the pup that is neither the boldest nor the shyest in the litter. Since the breeder has had more time to get to know the puppies' personalities, consider his or her opinion seriously. Many people who can't decide let the puppy pick them. It's hard to say no to a little tyke that bounces over to say hello and ends up nibbling your fingers and falling asleep in your lap. Of course you may be in big trouble if you end up with a whole lap full!

By eight weeks of age, JRT puppies should be curious and investigative. A puppy that freezes in place or always heads home when carried a short distance away from its littermates may not have the self-confidence of the typical Jack. Of course, one that constantly ignores you and prefers to run off and get into trouble may not be the best choice either. Part of the appeal of the Jack Russell Terrier is its mischievous personality, but don't be drawn to the troublemaker of the litter simply because he's so cute. Even the calmest of them will be mischievous enough!

## Good Looks

For *looks*, again consider the essentials of the Jack Russell Terrier standard. Your criteria will be more stringent if your pup is destined for a show career; in this case you should rely on the advice of the breeder, who will know better than anyone how dogs from that line mature.

# Adult Adoptees

Breeders may have adult dogs available that would relish the chance to live as a pampered pet. If you work away from home, have limited patience, or heirloom rugs, or if you demand a competition or breeding quality dog, consider an adult. Adults are often already housebroken and obedience trained, but don't count on this.

### The Rescue Jack

The rising popularity of the Jack Russell Terrier, combined with the tendency of people to underestimate the work involved in coexisting with a hunting terrier, has resulted in an overabundance of adult Jacks that have been given up by their first families. Some are advertised in the newspaper, some are forfeited to animal shelters, and some are fostered by JRT rescue organizations. They come in all descriptions and have varied histories, but the typical rescue Jack is a young adult whose human family found out they weren't up to owning an energetic and independent terrier. These dogs are just young Jacks acting like young Jacks; they need only to become part of a family who understands and appreciates their exuberance and need for mental and physical stimulation. A few come from traumatic backgrounds or may even be atypical

Jacks; these dogs are best adopted by experienced JRT owners. Good rescue groups will be able to tell which Jacks are typical and which are not. They carefully match prospective adoptees with their new homes, increasing their chances of finding a home for life.

Before adopting a rescue dog, find out as much as you can about its background, the reason it was given up, how it relates to men, women, children, and other pets, and any temperament or health problems it may have.

*Sometimes it's hard to go wrong...*

## Chapter Three

# True to Form

Jack Russell Terriers can be beautiful in many ways. A dog that emerges from a den covered with grime and exuding pride at a job well done epitomizes the beauty of the breed for many people. For others, real beauty lies in the everyday antics and companionship of a best friend. Still others are enraptured by the esthetics of a beautifully formed and balanced athlete. To the true JRT enthusiast, the most beautiful dog combines beauty of temperament, function, health, and appearance.

## Form and Function

The Jack Russell Terrier, like other dogs bred to face their quarry underground, must have certain mental and physical traits to enable him to do so. Paramount is intelligence, courage, and persistence. These cannot be evaluated in the ring, or for that matter, anywhere but in the field. An earthdog relies on its nose to identify an occupied den and locate its inhabitant within; again, this cannot be evaluated in the show ring. However, some attributes can be evaluated at a

*The JRT is built tough to do a tough job.*

dog show. The dog must be small enough to enter a den, yet large enough to effectively stand off its inhabitant. Long-legged dogs can crawl through a tunnel, so the limiting size factor tends to be the circumference of the chest. A chest with the circumference of a man's two hands is considered ideal for fox hunting terriers. In addition, if the dog is held up so that its front feet extend beyond its chest and its elbows are pushed together, the front legs should lie parallel against each other in a dog unless the chest is too wide, in which case they tend to cross. Flexibility is another essential trait for a dog that must maneuver in tight spaces. The coat and skin of an earthdog must be tough and resistant to water and teeth as much as possible. The jaws must be strong, the eyes protected in their sockets, the ear canals protected from falling dirt, and the limbs strong and well-muscled.

### The Parson's Perfect Terrier

The Parson Russell described his ideal terrier in 1871:

> "A small energetic terrier of from 14–16 pounds in weight, standing about 14 inches at the

withers, legs straight as arrows; a thick skin, a good rough weather-resisting coat, thick, close; and a trifle wiry, well calculated to protect the body from cold and wet, but with no affinity to the wiry jacket of the Scotch Terrier. It is certain that a good horse or dog cannot be a bad color, but I prefer a white dog. The bitch 'Trump' was white with just a patch of dark over each eye and ear, with a similar dot not larger than a penny-piece at the root of the tail. Feet should be perfect, the loins and conformation of the whole frame indicative of hardihood and endurance. The size and height of the animal may be compared to a fully grown vixen. Every inch a sportsman, the dog must not be quarrelsome. As regards height, some people prefer them to be rather more on the leg if they are to run with the hounds all day."

Through the years the breed has taken on certain characteristics that stamp its members as Jack Russell Terriers, some of which may be of more esthetic and historical value than functional. The breed standard is the measuring stick by which Jack Russell Terriers are judged in the show ring. Ideally, it describes the terrier that could best perform its job in the field and be identified with traditional points of JRT type. Several breed standards exist for the JRT. This, combined with the wide variety in size, coat, and type that is acceptable within the more popular of these standards, allows for great variation within the breed. This variability is one of the breed's attributes, allowing for specialization within the breed for hunting different quarry over different terrain.

The original JRT standard was drafted in 1904 by the founder of the Parson Jack Russell Club, Arthur Heinemann, and most current JRT standards are modeled more or less based on Heinemann's version. In the United States, the breed is usually judged by either the AKC or the JRTCA standard. Both

*The ideal JRT is of sound body and mind.*

### Terrier Terms

- **Angulation:** in the rear, angles formed between the pelvis, stifle, and hock; in the forequarters, angles formed between the shoulder blade, upper arm, and leg
- **Brindle:** color pattern in which lighter hairs are overlaid with vertical streaks of black hairs, creating a tiger stripe effect
- **Drive:** extent to which the legs, particularly the rear legs, push off when trotting
- **Grizzle:** color pattern in which each hair is banded and tipped with darker hair
- **Hare feet:** long, narrow feet
- **Hound ear:** large, hanging ear
- **Occiput:** rearmost point of the backskull
- **Overshot:** malocclusion in which the upper jaw extends beyond the lower jaw, creating a gap between the incisors.
- **Prick ears:** ears that stand up without folding
- **Reach:** extent to which the legs, particularly the front legs, move forward when trotting
- **Sparring:** facing off two dogs in the ring so they will challenge each other
- **Stifle:** knee
- **Stop:** transition point between the forehead and muzzle
- **Undershot:** malocclusion in which the lower jaw extends beyond the upper jaw, so that the bottom incisors are in front of the top incisors
- **Withers:** highest point over the shoulder blades
- **Wry mouth:** malocclusion in which only one side of the jaw is overshot or undershot

standards describe the same tough and lively hunter, but with some subtle differences.

# The JRTAA/AKC Standard of Perfection

**General Appearance:** The Jack Russell Terrier was developed in the south of England in the 1800s as a white terrier to work European red fox both above and below ground. The terrier was named for the Reverend John Russell, whose terriers trailed hounds and bolted foxes from dens so the hunt could ride on.

To function as a working terrier, he must possess certain characteristics: a ready attitude, alert and confident; balance in height and length; medium in size and bone, suggesting strength and endurance. Important to breed type is a natural appearance: harsh, weatherproof coat with a compact construction and clean silhouette. The coat is broken or smooth. He has a small, flexible

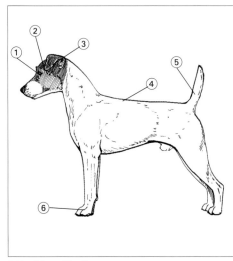

# Illustrated Standard

① Almond-shaped eyes
② Skull flat
③ Button ears; small V-shaped drop ear carried forward with the tip pointing toward the eye
④ Topline straight, with loin slightly arched
⑤ Tail set high and carried gaily; docked so tip is about level with skull
⑥ Cat feet

❏ **Color:** predominantly white with tan, black, or brown markings
❏ **DQ:** under 12" or over 15" tall; prick ears; liver nose; four or more missing teeth; overshot, undershot, or wry mouth; brindle markings; overt aggression toward dogs or humans

*DQ = Disqualification

chest to enable him to pursue his quarry underground and sufficient length of leg to follow the hounds. Old scars and injuries, the result of honorable work or accident, should not be allowed to prejudice a terrier's chance in the show ring, unless they interfere with movement or utility for work or breeding.

**Size, Proportion, Substance:** Size—both sexes are properly balanced between 12 and 14 inches (30 and 32 cm) at the withers. The ideal height of a mature dog is 14 inches (35 cm) at the withers, and bitches 13 inches (32 cm). Terriers whose heights measure either slightly larger or smaller than the ideal are not to be penalized in the show ring provided other points of their conformation, especially balance and chest span, are consistent with the breed standard. The weight of a terrier in hard working condition is usually 13 to 17 lbs (6–8 kg).

Proportion—balance is the keystone of the terrier's anatomy. The chief points of consideration are the relative proportions of skull and foreface, head and frame, height at withers, and length of body. The height at withers is slightly greater than the distance from withers to tail (e.g., by possibly 1 to 1½ inches [2.5–4 cm] on a 14-inch [35-cm] dog). The measurement will vary according to height, the ratio of height to back being approximately 6:5.

Substance—the terrier is of medium bone, not so heavy as to appear coarse or so light as to appear racy. The conformation of the whole frame is indicative of strength and endurance.

Disqualification: height under 12 inches (30 cm) or over 15 inches (37 cm).

**Head:** Head—strong and in good proportion to the rest of the body, so the appearance of balance is maintained. Expression—keen, direct, full of life and intelligence. Eyes—almond shaped, dark in color, moderate in size, not protruding. Dark rims are desirable. Ears—button ear. Small "V" shaped drop ears of moderate thickness carried forward close to the head with the tip so as to cover the orifice and pointing toward the eye. Fold is level with the top of the skull or slightly above. When alert, ear tips do not extend below the corner of the eye. Skull—flat and fairly broad between the ears, narrowing slightly to the eyes. The stop is well defined but not prominent. Muzzle—length from nose to stop is slightly shorter than the distance from stop to occiput. Jaws—upper

and lower are of fair and punishing strength. Nose—Must be black and fully pigmented. Bite—teeth are large with complete dentition in a perfect scissors bite (i.e., upper teeth closely overlapping the lower teeth and teeth set square to the jaws).

Faults: light or yellow eye, round eye; hound ear, fleshy ear, rounded tips.

Disqualifications: prick ears; liver color nose; four or more missing teeth; overshot, undershot, or wry mouth.

**Neck, Topline, Body:** Neck—clean and muscular, moderately arched, of fair length, gradually widening so as to blend well into the shoulders. Topline—strong, straight, and level in motion, the loin slightly

*Level bite. A scissors bite occurs when the top incisors slightly overlap the bottom incisors.*

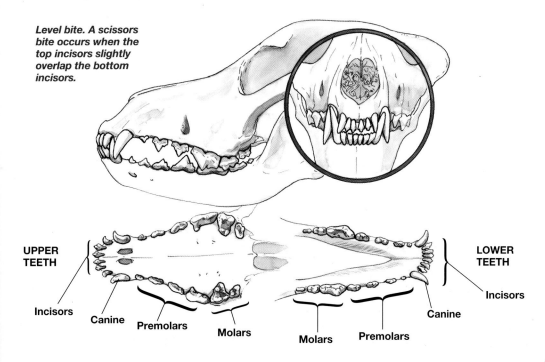

UPPER TEETH

LOWER TEETH

Incisors

Incisors

Canine

Premolars

Molars

Molars

Premolars

Canine

*"Expression: keen, direct, full of life and intelligence." (AKC standard).*

*The broken coat has only a hint of eyebrows and beard.*

arched. Body—in overall length to height proportion, the dog appears approximately square and balanced. The back is neither short nor long. The back gives no appearance of slackness but is laterally flexible, so that he may turn around in an earth. Tuck-up is moderate. Chest—narrow and of moderate depth, giving an athletic rather than heavily-chested appearance; must be flexible and compressible. The ribs are fairly well sprung, oval rather than round, not extending past the level of the elbow. Tail—set high, strong, carried gaily but not over the back or curled. Docked so the tip is approximately level to the skull, providing a good handhold. Faults: chest not spannable or shallow; barrel ribs; tail set low or carried over the back (squirrel tail).

**Forequarters:** Shoulders—long and sloping, well laid back, cleanly cut at the withers. Point of shoulder sits in a plane behind the point of the prosternum. The shoulder blade and upper arm are of approximately the same length; forelegs are placed well under the dog. Elbows—hang perpendicular to the body, working free of the sides. Legs are strong and straight with good bone. Joints turn neither in nor out. Pasterns—firm and nearly straight. Feet—round, catlike, very compact, the pads thick and tough, the toes moderately arched pointing forward, turned neither in nor out. Fault: hare feet.

**Hindquarters**—strong and muscular, smoothly molded, with good angulation and bend of stifle. Hocks near the ground, parallel, and driving in action. Feet as in front.

**Coat:** Smooth—double-coated. Coarse and weatherproof. Flat but hard, dense and abundant, belly and undersides of thighs are not bare. Broken—double-coated. Coarse and weatherproof. Short, dense undercoat covered with a harsh, straight, tight jacket, which lies flat and close to the body and legs. There is a clear outline with only a hint of eyebrows and beard. Belly and undersides of thighs are not bare. Coat does not show a strong tendency to curl or wave. No sculpted furnishings. The terrier is shown in his natural appearance, not excessively groomed. Sculpturing is to be severely penalized. Faults: soft, silky, wooly, or curly topcoat; lacking undercoat.

**Color**: White, white with black or tan markings, or a combination of these, tri-color. Colors are clear. Markings are preferably confined to the head and root of tail. Heavy body markings are not desirable. Grizzle is acceptable and should not be confused with brindle. Disqualification: brindle markings.

**Gait:** Movement or action is the crucial test of conformation. The terrier's movement is free, lively, well coordinated, with straight action in front and behind. There should be ample reach and drive with a good length of stride.

**Character and Temperament:** Bold and friendly. Athletic and clever. At work he is a game hunter, tenacious and courageous. At home he is playful, exuberant, and overwhelmingly affectionate. He is an independent and energetic terrier and requires his due portion of attention. He should not be quarrelsome. Shyness should not be confused with submissiveness. Submissiveness is not a fault. Sparring is not acceptable. Fault: shyness. Disqualification: overt aggression towards another dog or human.

**Spanning:** To measure a terrier's chest, span from behind, raising only the front feet from the ground, and compress gently. Directly behind the elbows is the smaller, firm part of the chest. The central part is usually larger but should feel rather elastic. Span with hands tightly behind the elbows on the forward portion of the chest. The chest must be easily spanned by average size hands. Thumbs should meet at the spine and fingers should meet under the chest. This is a significant factor and a critical part of the judging process. The dog cannot be correctly judged without this procedure.

**Disqualifications:** height under 12 inches (30 cm) or over 15 inches (37 cm); prick ears; liver nose; four or more missing teeth; overshot, undershot, or wry mouth; brindle markings; overt aggression towards other dogs or humans.

# The JRTCA Standard of Perfection

**Characteristics:** The terrier must present a lively, active, and alert appearance. It should impress you with its fearless and happy disposition. It should be remembered that the Jack Russell is a working terrier

*The English Jack Russell Terrier stands only 8 to 12 inches high, and is slightly longer than tall.*

and should retain these instincts. Nervousness, cowardice, or overaggressiveness should be discouraged, and it should always appear confident.

**General Appearance:** A sturdy, tough terrier, very much on its toes all of the time, measuring between 10 inches and 15 inches (25–38 cm) at the withers. The body length must be in proportion to the height, and it should present a compact, balanced image, always being in solid, hard condition.

**Head:** Should be well-balanced and in proportion to the body. The skull should be flat, of moderate width at the ears, narrowing to the eyes. There should be a defined stop but not overly pronounced. The length of muzzle from the nose to the stop should be slightly shorter than the distance from the stop to the

occiput. The nose should be black. The jaw should be powerful and well boned with strongly muscled cheeks.

**Eyes:** Should be almond shaped, dark in color, and full of life and intelligence.

**Ears:** Small V-shaped drop ears carried forward close to the head and of moderate thickness.

**Mouth:** Strong teeth with the top slightly overlapping the lower. (*Note:* A level bite is acceptable for registration.)

**Neck:** Clean and muscular, of good length, gradually widening at the shoulders.

**Forequarters:** The shoulders should be sloping and well laid back, fine at points, and clearly cut at the withers. Forelegs should be strong and straight-boned with joints in correct alignment. The elbows should

**The English Jack Russell Terrier Club Alliance (EJRTCA) Standard**

**Height:** The height of the terrier shall be between 8 and 12 inches (20–30 cm) as measured at the withers with the dog standing fully erect.

**Body:** Sturdy, balanced terrier. Body length slightly longer than length of leg. Length should not exceed function. Straight back with high tail carried erect. Chest should be spannable by two hands behind the shoulder blades. The rear should be well put together with strong muscle and good an angulation. Well laid back shoulder.

**Neck:** Well laid into shoulder.

**Head:** Strong boned with powerful jaws and strong cheek muscles. Dark almond-shaped eyes, pigmented eye rims, dark black pigment on nose. Small, V-shaped ears carried close to the head. Prick, semi-prick, and rose ears are acceptable but not preferred.

**Teeth:** The points of the upper incisors slightly overlapping the lower. May be missing up to four teeth.

**Legs:** Straight as is consistent with the short legs for which we aim.

**Feet:** Houndlike, foxlike, and harelike are all acceptable. All three are considered sound working feet for a Jack Russell.

**Gait:** Free, lively, well coordinated.

**Coat:** Smooth, rough or broken without coat being wooly. Smooth should not be sparse. Belly and underside coated.

**Color:** Predominantly white with tan, black, or brown markings. Ticked or mottled acceptable. Brindle not acceptable.

**Faults:** Nervousness, cowardice, overaggressiveness, weak bite, unsound movement, minor physical deformities.

**Disqualifications:** Extreme viciousness, shyness, or major physical deformities (these are considered such serious traits that dogs having them are not to be used for breeding). Undershot or overshot bites, wry mouth.

---

be hanging perpendicular to the body and working free of the sides.

**Body:** The chest should be shallow and narrow, and the front legs set not too widely apart, giving an athletic, rather than heavily chested, appearance. As a guide only, the chest should be small enough to be easily spanned behind the shoulders, by average-size hands, when the terrier is in a fit, working condition. The back should be strong, straight and, in comparison to the height of the terrier, give a balanced image. The loin should be slightly arched.

> ☆ **JACK FACT** ☆
>
> **English Jack Russell Terrier Club Alliance (EJRTCA) Registration**
>
> Dogs are registered with the EJRTCA at three levels:
>
> • **Advanced:** The dog meets or exceeds the EJRTCA standard and has a three-generation pedigree; or, a dog has advanced from the "Tentative" level based on show or trial performance.
>
> • **Tentative:** The dog meets the EJRTCA standards but lacks a three-generation pedigree.
>
> • **Pet Quality:** The dog basically meets the EJRTCA standard but has one or more faults that make it unsuitable for breeding, or a dog that has been spayed or neutered.

**Hindquarters:** Strong and muscular, well put together with good angulation and bend of stifle, giving plenty of drive and propulsion. Seen from behind, the hocks must be straight.

**Feet:** Round, hard-padded, of catlike appearance, neither turning in nor out.

**Tail:** Should be set rather high, carried gaily and in proportion to body length, usually about 4 inches (10 cm) long, providing a good hand hold.

**Coat:** Smooth, without being so sparse as to not provide a certain amount of protection from the elements and undergrowth. Rough or broken coated, without being wooly.

**Color:** White should predominate (i.e., coat must be more than 51 percent white) with tan, black, or brown markings. Brindle markings are unacceptable.

**Gait:** Movement should be free, lively, and well coordinated with straight action in front and behind.

**Special Notes:** Old scars or injuries, the result of work or accident, should not be allowed to prejudice a terrier's chance in the show ring unless they interfere with its movement or with its utility for work or stud.

A Jack Russell Terrier should not show any strong characteristics of another breed.

**Faults:**

- shyness
- disinterest
- overaggression
- defects in bite
- weak jaws
- fleshy ears
- down at the shoulder
- barrel ribs
- out at elbow
- narrow hips
- straight stifles
- weak feet
- sluggish or unsound movement
- dishing
- plaiting
- toeing
- silky or wooly coats
- too much color (less than 51 percent white)
- shrill or weak voice
- lack of muscle or skin tone
- lack of stamina or lung reserve
- evidence of foreign blood

# The Standards Compared

Both standards emphasize the working abilities of the Jack Russell Terrier, and call for an athletic dog without exaggeration. A couple of discrepancies between the two standards have created some controversy, however.

**Size:** The AKC standard states that "both sexes are properly balanced between 12 inches and 14 inches (30–35 cm) at the withers. The ideal height of a mature dog is 14 inches (35 cm) at the withers, and bitches 13 inches (32 cm). Terriers whose heights measure either slightly larger or smaller than the ideal are not to be penalized..." whereas the JRTCA standard calls for height between 10 inches and 15 inches (25–37 cm). The JRTCA divides the breed for purposes of showing into a 10 inches to 12½ inches (25–31 cm) class and an over 12½ inches to 15 inches (31–37 cm) class. The AKC disqualifies dogs under 12 inches (30 cm) or over 15 inches (37 cm), which would include a large percentage of dogs in the lower JRTCA division.

**Proportion:** The AKC standard states that the "height at the withers is slightly greater than the distance from the withers to tail (e.g., possibly by 1½ inches (4 cm) on a 14-inch (35-cm) dog. The measurement will vary according to height, the ratio of height to back being approximately 6:5." The JRTCA standard does not explicitly describe the correct pro-

*Good looking by any standard.*

portions; some fanciers believe, however, that the description provided by the AKC standard promotes a shorter backed dog.

**Color:** The AKC standard states, "Markings are preferably confined to the head and root of the tail. Heavy body markings are not desirable." The JRTCA standard requires only that "White should predominate (i.e., must be more than 51 percent white)..." The AKC standard disqualifies a liver nose, while the JRTCA simply states the nose should be black. The AKC standard states that

*Which registry for me?*

# JRTCA Registration

Unlike pedigree-based registries, the JRTCA registers dogs on an individual application basis. Each dog must meet certain requirements of breeding, type, and health in order to be registered with the JRTCA. Dogs applying for registration must be over one year of age and be owned by a member of the JRTCA. The JRTCA will not allow into its membership anyone who registers their JRT with any conflicting kennel club, including the American Kennel Club or the United Kennel Club. Dogs failing in some requirements may not be registered, but can still be recorded, which enables them to compete in JRTCA hunting trials. However, JRT's under 10 inches or over 15 inches in height at the withers are ineligible for JRTCA registration or recording. Applications for registration must include:

• **Stud service certificate** signed by the owner of the dog's sire.

• **Four generation pedigree.** Products of inbreedings (mother/son, father/daughter, brother/sister) are not acceptable, and half sister/half brother matings are allowable only once in every three generations.

• **Official JRTCA veterinary certificate.** Dogs must be clear of defects of possible hereditary nature, such as cryptorchidism, eye problems, bite problems, luxated patellas, and some hernias. A spay/neuter certificate will suffice in place of a veterinary certificate.

dark eye rims are desirable, whereas the JRTCA standard does not mention a preference.

**Disqualifications:** The AKC standard lists several disqualifications that render a dog ineligible for conformation competition. The JRTCA does not include disqualifications as part of its standard. However, because of the process of JRTCA registration, dogs with some traits are effectively disqualified by excluding them from full registration. Jacks under 10 inches (25 cm) and over 15 inches (37 cm), for example, are refused JRTCA registration or recording privileges.

• **Color photographs.** Dogs must be evaluated from the front and both sides to ensure that they generally adhere to the breed standard. The photos must be signed by the veterinarian at the time the veterinary health certificate is signed.

# AKC Registration

The AKC registers dogs according to evidence of pure breeding, which means that to receive full AKC registration both parents should be registered with the AKC or another registry recognized by the AKC. The JRTCA is not among the AKC recognized registries. However, you can obtain an Indefinite Listing Privilege (ILP) registration number for a dog that looks sufficiently like a Jack Russell Terrier even though it may lack pedigree credentials, as long as the dog is spayed or neutered. An ILP number will enable your dog to compete in all AKC events for which JRT's are usually eligible except for conformation shows.

Unfortunately, under current circumstances, it is not possible to have dual (AKC and JRTCA) registered dogs or to compete at both JRTCA and AKC events. This schism results from an earnest disagreement about what is best for the breed's future; but all the dogs know is that they want to go have fun anywhere, whether it's AKC, JRTCA, or your backyard!

*The organization that you register your JRT with will determine which events your dog can compete in.*

## Chapter Four

# Terrier Diets

Every day you place a bowl down in front of your dog filled with food that influences her performance, health, and longevity, as well as her dining pleasure. While the same can be said of human meals, dog diets differ from human diets in that most dogs are usually fed only a single type of food day in and day out. This makes choosing the best diet even more important, intimidating, and controversial. The first point of contention is whether dogs are better off being fed commercially prepared diets or home prepared diets.

## Raw, Cooked, or Processed?

For thousands of years wild canids ate a diet consisting largely of raw meat as well as whatever vegetables were contained in their prey's stomach contents. Early domesticated dogs subsisted largely on human garbage as well as whatever they could catch or forage themselves. For many centuries domestic dogs' diets were leftovers, scraps, and bread products.

*Your Jack is what he eats.*

## Commercial Diets

Only in recent decades have commercial foods been available, complete with testing of their nutritional value. Proponents of commercial foods point out that these diets have been constantly adjusted and tested on generations of dogs to provide optimal nutrition, and that premium grade foods contain human quality ingredients. Critics of commercial foods point out that these foods are highly processed, do not resemble a dog's natural diet, are not fresh, and may use ingredients unfit for human consumption.

## Raw Food

A recently popularized alternative to commercial diets are raw food diets. These diets advocate more natural feeding by giving dogs whole raw animal carcasses, particularly chicken, which the dog eats bones and all. Proponents point out that such diets are more like the natural diet of ancestral dogs, and claim good health, clean teeth, and economical food bills. Controlled studies on the safety and efficacy of such diets have yet to be published.

Detractors point out that, while the raw diet may be closer to what wolves eat, dogs are no longer wolves and haven't lived off the land for thousands of generations. In addition, many people have oversimplified these diets and commonly feed an exclusive diet of chicken wings, which is neither natural nor balanced. Critics also worry that raw foods from processing plants may pose the threat of *salmonella* and *E. coli* bacteria, although dogs are more resistant to illness from them compared to people. If raw food is fed it should only be fresh and locally processed.

A third, and perhaps the best, alternative is to cook homemade diets according to recipes devised by canine nutritionists. Such diets provide a variety of nutrients in fresh foods according to accepted nutrition standards for dogs, but they are more labor intensive than other choices. Ask your veterinarian to suggest a source for home prepared menus.

## A Varied Diet

Most dogs, unless they've been raised on only one food, prefer a varied menu, and varying a dog's diet can provide some insurance that it's getting proper nutrition by providing a wide range of ingredients. In fact, dogs tend to prefer a novel food, but then tire of it within a few days. However, many dogs develop diarrhea from abrupt changes in diet, so you must change foods gradually with these dogs. It is a tribute to the dog's general hardiness that most dogs survive under any of these feeding schemes. But for your Jack to be all that she can be you may have to do

*Yum, yum...*

some experimenting and understand some basics of canine nutrition.

# Evaluating Foods

Dogs are omnivorous, meaning their nutritional needs can best be met by a diet derived from both animals and plants. These nutrients are commercially available in several forms. Dry food (containing about 10 percent moisture) is the most popular, economical, and healthy, but least enticing form of dog food. Semi-moist foods (with about 30 percent moisture) contain high levels of sugar used as preservatives. They are tasty, convenient, and very handy for traveling, but are not an optimal nutritional choice as a regular diet. Canned food has a high moisture content (about 75 percent), which helps to make them tasty, but it also makes them comparatively expensive, because you're essentially buying water.

If you choose to feed commercial food, feed a high quality food from a name-brand company that states it meets the recommended minimal nutrient levels for dogs set by the

*Your JRT depends on you to serve a nutritious, tasty meal.*

Association of American Feed Control Officials (AAFCO) and has been tested through actual feeding trials. Always strive to buy and use only the freshest food available. Dry food loses nutrients as it sits, and the fat content can become rancid.

# Canine Nutrition

When comparing food labels, keep in mind that differences in moisture content make it difficult to make direct comparisons between the guaranteed analyses in different forms of food unless you first do some calculations to equate the percentage of dry matter food. A good rule of thumb is that three or four of the first six ingredients of a dog food should be animal derived. These tend to be tastier and more highly digestible than plant based ingredients; more highly digestible foods generally mean less stool volume and less gas problems. The components that vary most from one brand to another are protein and fat percentages.

## Protein

Protein provides the necessary building blocks for growth and maintenance of bones, muscle, and coat, and in the production of infection fighting antibodies. The quality of protein is as important as its quantity. Meat-derived protein is higher quality and more highly digestible than plant derived protein. This means that two foods with identical protein percentages can differ in the nutritional level of protein according to the protein's source.

Stressed, highly active, or underweight dogs should be fed higher protein levels. Puppies, as well as pregnant and nursing mothers, need particularly high protein and somewhat higher fat levels in their diets, such as the levels found in puppy foods. It used to be thought that older dogs should be fed low protein diets in order to avoid kidney problems, but it's now known that high protein diets do not cause kidney failure. In fact, high quality protein is essential to dogs with compromised kidney function. Such dogs should have reduced phosphorous levels, however, and special diets are available that satisfy these requirements. Most adult Jacks will do fine on regular adult foods having protein levels of about 20 to 22 percent (dry food percentage).

## Fat

Fat is the calorie-rich component of foods, and most dogs prefer the taste of foods with higher fat content. Fat is necessary to good health, aiding in the transport of important vitamins and providing energy. Dogs deficient in fat (usually from diets containing less than 5 percent dry matter fat) may have sparse, dry coats and scaly skin. Excessive fat intake can cause obesity and appetite reduction, creating a deficiency in other nutrients. Working dogs usually need a high fat diet to meet their high energy requirements. Obese dogs or dogs with heart problems, pancreatitis, or diarrhea should be fed a low fat food.

## Carbohydrates

Carbohydrates in most dog foods are primarily plant derived.

---

### ☆ JACK FACT ☆

**Diarrhea**

Diarrhea can result from excitement, nervousness, a change in diet or water, sensitivity to certain foods, overeating, intestinal parasites, viral or bacterial infections, or ingestion of toxic substances. Its consistency, color, and contents (parasites, blood, mucus, or foreign objects) are all clues of the severity and possible causes of your dog's problem. You can treat mild diarrhea by withholding or severely restricting food and water for 24 hours. Ice cubes can be given to satisfy thirst. Administer human diarrhea medication in the same weight dosage as recommended for humans. Feed a bland diet consisting of rice, tapioca, or cooked macaroni, along with cottage cheese or tofu for protein. Note that dogs with some concurrent illnesses may not be candidates for food or water restriction. Diarrhea with vomiting, fever, or other signs of toxicity, or diarrhea that lasts for more than a day or that is bloody, should not be allowed to continue without seeking veterinary advice.

---

They are a fairly inexpensive source of nutrition and make up a large part of most commercial dog foods. Many carbohydrates are poorly utilized by the dogs' digestive system. Those derived from rice are best utilized, those from potato and corn

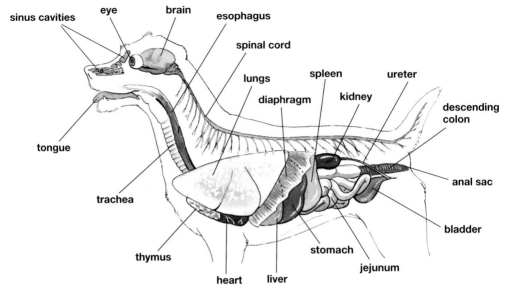

**Internal anatomy.**

far less so, and wheat, oat, and beans even less again. Cooking increases the nutrient availability. Excessive amounts of carbohydrates in the diet can cause decreased performance, diarrhea, and flatulence.

### Fiber

Fiber in dog food varies considerably. Better quality fiber sources include beet pulp and rice bran, but even these should provide a small percentage of a food's ingredients. Weight reducing diets often include larger amounts of fiber so the dog will feel more full and to prevent digestibility of some of the other nutrients. Too much fiber interferes with digestion and can cause diarrhea or larger stool volume.

### Optimal Nutrient Levels

A dog's optimal level of each nutrient will change according to its age, energy requirements, and state of health. Prescription commercial diets and recipes for home prepared diets are available for dogs with various illnesses or needs.

---

### ☆ JACK FACT ☆

**Water**

Water is essential for your dog's health and comfort. Don't just keep your dog's water bowl full by topping it up every day. Such a habit allows algae to form along the sides of the bowl, and gives bacteria a chance to multiply. Empty, scrub, and refill the water bowl daily.

---

*"What's for supper?"*

## SPECIAL DIETS

Several diseases can be adversely affected by feeding some normal dog food ingredients; conversely, sometimes the effects of these disorders can be mitigated by diet. Commercial diets are available for most major diseases that are influenced by diet, and home-prepared recipes are also available. Many dogs tire of these diets, however, and owners often supplement with treats that offset the proper nutrition of the special diets. Understanding the dietary requirements can help you choose proper foods for an affected dog. Any restricted diet should be undertaken only under veterinary advice, which is why most commercial diets of this nature are available only through veterinarians.

**Congestive Heart Failure:** Feeding a low sodium diet is the foremost dietary requirement for dogs with congestive heart failure. Some dogs also require slightly higher levels of potassium and magnesium. Because kidney failure often occurs in conjunction with heart failure, finding a palatable diet is often difficult; this, combined with the wasting effect of heart failure and the appetite reducing side effects of some cardiac medications, makes it a challenge to keep adequate weight on these dogs. Vitamin B12 may stimulate the appetite slightly.

**Chronic Renal Disease:** Kidney disease is one of the more common problems of older dogs. It is progressive and irreversible. The role of protein in management of chronic renal disease remains controversial, and it varies with the individual dog. Feeding a low protein diet reduces the work the nephrons of the kidney must do by reducing toxic protein waste products. High quality protein has less toxic waste products, so that the dog obtains the beneficial effects of protein while minimizing the adverse effects. Eggs have the highest quality protein, followed by milk, then beef or chicken, with about 75 percent the value of egg protein. Vegetable derived protein is even lower. The high sulfur content of eggs would contradict their use in dogs with marked acidosis, however, pointing to the fact that such diets cannot be designed without the input of veterinary tests and advice. A diet containing 8 to 10 percent high quality protein is usually good for dogs with renal disease. In addition, it is imperative that phosphorus intake be reduced, and calcium levels should be at least in a 1:1 ration to phosphorus. Salt should be restricted to control hypertension. Other ingredients may or may not need to be restricted or supplemented; obviously, designing an appropriate renal diet is something that requires an expert in veterinary nutrition.

**Liver Disease:** Dietary management is essential for dogs with liver disease. Of primary importance is that the dog must eat; fasting offers no opportunity for liver damage to recover. Meat should be avoided; preferable protein sources are milk, cottage cheese, or tofu. Simple and complex carbohydrates (such as rice, potatoes, and vegetables) are essential and should be fed in small, frequent meals throughout the day. The addition of fat can increase the

## SPECIAL DIETS (continued)

meal's tastiness. Vitamin B12 may be given to increase appetite. It is essential that Vitamin A be kept to a minimal level, and copper levels kept low.

**Urinary Stones:** Dogs can develop different kinds of urinary stones, and the choice of an appropriate diet depends upon the particular kind of stone. *Struvite calculi* are better treated with antibiotic therapy than dietary management. *Calcium oxalate calculi* are best prevented with diets low in oxalate and calcium, minimal vitamin D, normal phosphorus levels, and high levels of magnesium and citrate. *Urate calculi* are best managed with diets low in purine, and diets that also encourage increased water consumption.

**Diabetes Mellitus:** A diet high in complex carbohydrates, low fat, moderate protein, and no simple sugars is suggested for diabetic dogs. The feeding schedule is equally important for these dogs. Designing a successful feeding regime for a diabetic dog will require significant commitment and teamwork with your veterinarian.

**Food Allergies:** Symptoms of food allergies range from diarrhea to itchy skin and ears. If you suspect your dog has a food allergy, consult your veterinarian about an elimination diet, in which you start with a bland diet consisting of ingredients your dog has never eaten before. Lamb and rice foods used to be vigorously promoted as hypoallergenic, but because a dog is now likely to have eaten lamb previously, that is no longer true. Your veterinarian can suggest sources of protein (such as venison, duck, or rab-

bit) that your dog will probably not have eaten previously. You may have to keep the dog on this diet for at least a month, withholding treats, pills, and even toys that might be creating an allergic response. If the symptoms go away, then ingredients are added back to the diet gradually, or a novel commercial diet is tried. It may take a lot of experimentation, but a healthy and happy dog will be well worth it.

**Pancreatitis:** Pancreatitis is more common in older or middle aged dogs, especially overweight ones. It is often precipitated by a high fat meal, and is the most common illness associated with Thanksgiving and Christmas. Symptoms include lack of appetite, lethargy, and signs of abdominal discomfort (such as standing with front legs down on the ground in a bowing position), and possibly vomiting, diarrhea, and even shock or death. Although most dogs can eat a high fat meal without a problem, once a dog develops pancreatitis, a high fat meal often precipitates subsequent episodes.

# Feeding and Weight

Adult dogs can be fed once a day, but it's usually better to feed smaller meals twice a day. Very young puppies should be fed three or four times a day, on a regular schedule. Feed them as much as they care to eat in about 15 minutes. From the age of three to six months, pups should be fed three times daily, and after that, twice daily.

It's seldom a good idea to let a JRT self-feed by leaving food available at all times. Food that is wet can spoil and some dogs will over-indulge. By feeding discreet meals you can get a good idea if your dog is eating as she should be.

Your dog's weight is the best gauge of how much more or less you should be feeding. All dogs have different metabolism, so each dog's diet must be adjusted accordingly. The Jack Russell Terrier is an athlete, and should have a lean, muscular body. The ribs should be easily felt through a layer of muscle, but they should not be visible. There should be no roll of fat over the withers or rump, but neither the backbone nor the hip bones should be prominent. Viewed both in profile and from above, the JRT should have an hourglass figure.

## Weight Reduction Diets

A fat Jack Russell Terrier can't fully enjoy many of the activities this breed lives for—and besides, a fat Jack could get stuck in a hole! Obesity predisposes dogs to joint injuries and heart problems and makes many preexisting problems worse.

Your dog's health should be checked by your veterinarian before embarking on any serious weight reduction effort. Heart disease and some endocrine disorders, such as hypothyroidism or Cushing's disease, or the early stages of diabetes, can cause the appearance of obesity

---

## ☆ JACK FACT ☆

**Vomiting**

Consult your veterinarian immediately if your dog vomits a foul substance resembling fecal matter (indicating a blockage in the intestinal tract), blood (partially digested blood resembles coffee grounds), or if there is projectile or repeated vomiting. Repeated vomiting can result in dehydration, so if your dog can't hold anything down for a prolonged period it may have to get intravenous fluids. Other common causes of vomiting:

• Overeating, especially when followed by playing, often causes vomiting in puppies.

• Regurgitation immediately after meals can indicate an esophageal obstruction.

• Repeated vomiting can result from spoiled food, indigestible objects, or stomach illness.

Sporadic vomiting with poor appetite and generally poor condition could indicate internal parasites or a more serious internal disease.

---

and should be ruled out or treated. A dog in which only the stomach is enlarged, without fat around the shoulders or rump, is especially suspect and should be examined by a veterinarian.

Jacks that are simply overweight should be fed a lower calorie diet. The role of high fiber in reducing diets is controversial; recent studies suggest it does not provide the lowered hunger perception it was once thought to. Commercially available diet foods supply about 15 percent fewer calories per pound and are preferable to the alternative of just feeding less of a fattening food. Research indicates that protein levels should remain moderate to high in reducing diets in order to avoid the loss of muscle tissue. Home pre-pared diets are available that are both tasty and less fattening.

All those tasty treats you hand out during the day can add up to a significant number of calories in a small dog. But sharing treats is fun! Substitute a low calorie alternative such as rice cakes or carrots. Keep your dog out of the kitchen or dining area at food preparation and meal times. Schedule a walk immediately following your dinner to get your dog's mind off of your leftovers—it will be good for both of you.

## Weight Gaining Diets

A Jack that loses weight rapidly or steadily for no apparent reason should be taken to the veterinarian. Several diseases, including cancer, can cause wasting. A sick or

*Active dogs, like JRT's, require more calories in their diet.*

recuperating dog may have to be coaxed into eating. Cat food, meat baby food, and cooked meat are all relished by dogs and may entice a dog without an appetite to eat, but ask your veterinarian first.

A few dogs just don't gain weight well, and some are just picky eaters. Underweight dogs may gain weight with puppy food; add water, milk, bouillon, ground beef, or canned food and heat slightly to increase aroma and palatability. Milk will cause many dogs to have diarrhea, so try only a little bit at first. Of course, once you start this you know you're making your picky eater pickier!

# When Good Dogs Eat Bad Things

Dogs can eat a variety of strange and sometimes dangerous things. Small bones can become stuck across the roof of the mouth, causing the dog to claw frantically at his face. Sharp bone fragments and

## T E R R I E R   T E C H

### POISONING

Poisoning is always a concern with dogs. Some poisons are commonly found around the house, whereas others are more often found in fields and around barns—both places Jack Russells frequent when hunting. Signs of poisoning commonly include vomiting, convulsions, staggering, and collapse. If in doubt about whether poison was ingested, call the veterinarian anyway.

If the dog has ingested the poison within the past two hours, and is neither severely depressed, convulsing, or comatose, you may be advised to induce vomiting (unless the poison was an acid, alkali, petroleum product, solvent, cleaner, or tranquilizer). You can do this by giving either hydrogen peroxide (mixed 1:1 with water), salt water, or dry mustard and water.

In other cases you may be advised to dilute the poison by giving milk, vegetable oil, or egg whites. Activated charcoal can adsorb many toxins.

Baking soda or milk of magnesia can be given for ingested acids, and vinegar or lemon juice for ingested alkalis.

• Ethylene glycol-based antifreeze causes kidney failure; the prognosis is poor once symptoms appear. Veterinary treatment must be obtained within two to four hours of ingestion of even tiny amounts if the dog's life is to be saved.

• Warfarin-based rodent poisons contain anticoagulants that cause uncontrolled internal bleeding; the prognosis ranges from good (if caught soon after ingestion) to poor (if several days have elapsed).

• Cholecalciferol-based rodent poisons deposit calcium in the blood vessels causing kidney failure and other problems; the prognosis is poor even from eating small amounts.

• Strychnine-based squirrel and bird poisons (usually administered as bird other foreign objects can pierce parts of the digestive tract. Some foreign objects, and even rawhide chews, can cause blockage of the intestines. Particularly dangerous are long, stretchy objects, such as socks, that can pass into the intestines but then become lodged as the intestines become bunched around them accordian style. Such situations may need emergency surgery.

**Pica:** Pica, the ingestion of non-food items (such as wood, fabric, or soil) can be a problem in some dogs. Talk to your veterinarian about possible health problems that could contribute to this situation.

**Coprophagia:** The most common and disturbing non-food item eaten by dogs is feces. This habit, called coprophagia, has been blamed on boredom, stress, hunger, poor nutrition, and excessively rich nutrition. Food additives are available that make the stool less savory. The best cure is immediate removal of all feces.

## T E R R I E R   T E C H

### POISONING (continued)

seed with a blue coating of strychnine) can cause seizures, hyper-reactivity to noise, and rigid muscles. The prognosis is poor.

• Metaldehyde-based snail and slug poisons cause anxiety, unsteadiness, tremors, coma, and death; the prognosis is fair.

• Arsenic-based insect poisons, weed killers, and wood preservatives cause vomiting, diarrhea, and weakness, progressing to kidney failure, coma, and death; the prognosis is poor if symptoms have already started.

• Organophosphate-based flea and tick poisons and de-wormers, in overdose quantities, can cause vomiting, muscle tremors, pupil constriction, diarrhea, excitability, difficulty breathing, and death. The prognosis varies but can be poor.

• Theobromine (found in chocolate) can cause vomiting, diarrhea, restlessness, fever, seizures, coma, and death; toxic dose for dogs is 50 mg per pound of dog's weight. Dark chocolate contains over 400 mg/ounce, so a 2.5-ounce (70 mg) candy bar can be life threatening to a 20 lb. (9 kg) dog.

• Lead (found in paint, golf ball coatings, linoleum, and even newsprint) causes abnormal behavior, unsteadiness, seizures, loss of appetite, vomiting, diarrhea, and blindness. The prognosis is usually good.

• Zinc (found in pennies, zinc oxide skin cream, calamine lotion, fertilizers, and shampoos) causes breakdown of red blood cells. Symptoms include decreased appetite, vomiting, diarrhea, depression, pale gums, and brown urine. The prognosis is variable.

• Iron-based rose fertilizers can cause kidney and liver failure; toxic dose is 1 teaspoon of 5 percent concentration per 20-lb. (9-kg) dog. The prognosis is variable depending upon dosage and treatment delay.

# Chapter Five

# Beauty and the Beast

They don't call them dirt dogs for nothing. Jack Russells are happiest when they are making the dirt fly, and if some dirt, mud, or anything else gets on their coat, so much the better. Fortunately, most dirt and even mud (once dried) falls right out the Jack's harsh coat, but once in a while you need to step in and clean up your Jack.

Whether you have a smooth, rough, or broken-coated Jack, he will look and feel better if his coat is well groomed. Grooming is not only important for the sake of beauty; it also can prevent serious health problems. Just as with people, good grooming involves more than an occasional brushing of the hair. Keeping the nails, teeth, eyes, and ears well groomed is just as important, if not more so.

## The Jack Russell Jacket

The Jack Russell Terrier coat is relatively low maintenance. A quick once-over with a bristle brush or even

*Even a Jack Russell sometimes has to work at looking his best.*

a soft cloth will usually be enough to loosen dirt and impart a good sheen to the hair. Dogs kept indoors under artificial lighting shed year round, with a major shedding season in the spring. Not only is shed hair a nuisance around the house, but it can cause itching, and it gives the coat a dull, scraggly appearance. Many people contend the smooths shed the most, and it is probably true that these hairs fall off the dog with the greatest ease. A daily vigorous brushing during shedding season, using a stiff bristle brush, rubber curry brush, or slicker brush is the best way to hurry along shedding. More hairs will shed after bathing, and they are especially easy to dislodge when the hair is almost, but not quite yet, dry. Rough coats tend to hang in there a little longer and will need help in the form of plucking or stripping to dislodge dead hair.

### Casual Grooming

Casual grooming can be done with your dog seated beside you on a blanket, but if you're serious about your results, a grooming table is essential. Most come with a grooming arm from which hangs a leash (called a grooming noose) to hold the

The unkempt look does have a certain appeal, but lacks the dapper look of the plucked JRT.

dog still while grooming, freeing up both of your hands. Jacks are notorious for launching themselves off the table at the first opportunity, so you absolutely must not step away from it when your dog is being held by the noose, lest it act as a hangman's noose. A quick release safety clip allows for instant release of the noose in case of such an accident, and is a suggested accessory.

Begin grooming your Jack while he is still a puppy. Use plenty of treats and a soft brush. Reward him for standing calmly on the grooming table. Accustom him to being touched all over, and examine his feet, mouth, and ears. At this point his comfort and happiness in the situation is far more important than your grooming results.

# Stripping and Plucking

### The Stripping Process

Stripping refers to pulling out the dead hairs either by hand or with a stripping tool, whereas plucking more often refers to a type of stripping in which small groups of hairs are pulled out using the fingers only.

The longer hairs are not readily removed with regular brushing, which is better at dislodging the undercoat. Stripping and plucking your rough or broken-coated Jack during shedding season is the best way to keep your dog comfortable and dashing. If your dog has a longer coat, you may need additional stripping sessions through-out the year. Show dogs need to have maintenance stripping even more frequently.

## Tools

A stripping tool (or stripping knife or blade) is a serrated tool in which a sharp, cutting surface is between the small teeth. They come in various blade sizes, with the coarser ones better for heavy stripping and the finer ones more suitable for finishing touches. Because these blades tend to cut hairs, they don't yield quite as good results as hand plucking, but they are far easier on the groomer.

Some people find the prospect of plucking too tedious or strenuous. The process can be hard on arthritic fingers and some dogs are less than cooperative. If the coat is not too unwieldy, you can strip it using a coarse and then fine stripping comb. Although this tends to cut the coat in places, it still can give an attractive result. A stripping stone (a piece of coarse lava rock) can also help remove fine hairs.

## The Plucking Process

Test the coat to see if it is ready for plucking by grasping a few hairs and giving them a quick tug. If they don't pull out easily, then wait a week or two and try again.

Don't bathe your dog before plucking. Dirtier hair is less slick, and easier to grasp. Grooming chalk is available to make the hair even less slippery. Use the slicker brush to brush the hair in both directions to

remove as much loose hair as possible and help loosen the remaining hair. Apply the grooming chalk, then comb the hair backwards so that it stands off the body.

To pluck hair, hold the skin taut by pulling it with one hand. Use your index finger and thumb to grasp a few of the long hairs of the outer coat just above the shorter hairs of the undercoat (usually about an inch from the skin), and pull them sharply in the direction of hair growth. Begin where the hair is customarily longest, which is around the neck and ruff. Start at the top and work downward and rearward, but save the sensitive belly areas until last. Continue to comb the hair against its growth so you can pluck any straggling long hairs.

For a very thick coat, you can go over it with the stripping knife, but the results won't be quite as good as hand plucking. To use the stripping comb, place a few hairs between the comb and your thumb and pull in the direction of hair growth. Don't use wrist action! If you add a twisting motion, the comb will cut the hairs, which can lead to patches of overly short coat. After hand plucking, you can use the stripping comb around the neck area to blend it into the withers and chest. When using the stripping comb to give a final, neat appearance, comb it straight through the hair without any twisting motion.

The stripping knife may also be easier to use on a dog with thick growth on its legs. Most Jacks, however, will need very little plucking on their thighs and legs. The legs should not be bottle-brush legs, as seen on many wire coated terriers, but can still be left somewhat longer than on the body. Make sure they have a smooth outline, with no bumps over the pasterns. The feet should be neatened by first brushing the hair on the foot backwards so it stands away from the foot, then plucking out the longest hairs and finally using blunt nosed scissors to tidy up the hairs around the foot's perimeter.

**The tail:** The tail can be challenging, as you want it to look neither bushy nor whiplike. Use thinning scissors to give the tail tip a neat yet unsculpted appearance, leaving more or less hair depending on what best balances the dog's overall appearance. Use blunt scissors or thinning shears to trim carefully in the area around the underside near the dog's anus.

**The underside:** Be gentle on the dog's underside. It will be easier to get to if your dog lies on his back or if he is held so that he is standing on his hind legs. On males, use the blunt nosed scissors to trim around the penis sheath, rather than plucking the long hairs in that sensitive area. You can also use thinning shears to neaten up the underside.

**The face:** The face requires relatively little plucking. The eyebrow and whiskers are part of the breed's typical expression and should usually be left intact, unless uncharacteristically long. The only hair that normally needs to be plucked is the longer hair below the inner corners of the eyes, and possibly longer hairs that obscure the stop. Use the fine stripping comb to remove any longer hairs on top of the head, as well as longer hair on the sides of the head nearer the eyes, so that the wedge shape can be better appreciated.

## Time Requirements

A full grooming session can last several hours, which is more than most dogs (and groomers) can tolerate at one sitting. Take breaks and

*Some grooming can be done casually.*

don't make grooming an ordeal. By the same token, don't let the process linger on and on over many days. Plucking can be irritating to the skin, and it's a good idea after plucking to wash the dog in a soothing oatmeal or antimicrobial shampoo. However, since you don't want to bathe before plucking, this can be difficult if you are splitting up sessions over a long period. You can bathe and then use grooming chalk to again enable you to get a better grip for the next session, or bathe only the selected plucked areas.

Rather than wait until your dog becomes unkempt and then tackle a marathon stripping session, you can do what's called "rolling" the coat. In this technique you gently pinch up the skin between your thumb and index finger so that the skin is in a roll, which causes the longer hairs to stick out from the others. Pluck only these hairs. Go over the dog's entire body, repeating this. This allows you to pluck out longer hairs before they overwhelm you, and will keep your dog looking his best for as long as possible. If you plan to show your Jack you will want to roll his coat so that he can be shown with his coat in its best condition.

If possible, get an experienced JRT groomer to show you how to bring out the best in your particular dog. Don't put off your first attempt at show grooming until right before the show. Even then, you might want to do your first trims on the right side of the dog (the side the judge doesn't see much)—just in case you mess it up! Your JRT won't look his best until several weeks after being plucked, so don't put it off until the week before a big event.

Finally, don't do too perfect a job. JRT's should look like they just stepped out of the field rather than the beauty parlor. The finished JRT should have a neat outline to its body, but without the sculpted look seen in, for example, the Wire Fox Terrier. It should resemble a turned-out hunter rather than a caricature show dog.

# Bathing and Drying

You also can't put off bathing until just before a dog show. Bathing makes the coat too soft to be correct in competition, so it's better to bathe the dog several days to even a week before the event.

### Shampoo Selection

Texturizing and terrier coat shampoos are available that will help the coat stay harsh while still cleaning it. If you're not planning to compete with your dog you don't need a special shampoo, although it's still best to use a dog shampoo. Even the fanciest human shampoos aren't as good as these, because dogs and

*Puppies are mud magnets.*

human hair have different pH values and so need different shampoos. Dog skin has a pH of 7.5, while human skin has a pH of 5.5; bathing in a shampoo formulated for the pH of human skin can lead to scaling and irritation. If, however, your dog has a healthy coat and you just want a simple bath, using a human shampoo is fine. If you're on a budget and your dog has healthy skin and coat, a mild liquid dish washing detergent can actually give good results. Avoid shampoos with conditioners.

Some shampoos have whiteners and some have ingredients that claim to bring out the colors (the latter have very little, if any, such effect). Other shampoos are available from your veterinarian and are effective for various skin problems. Oatmeal based anti-pruritics can help soothe itchy skin, moisturizing shampoos can help with dry skin, anti-seborrheic shampoos can help with excessive greasy scaling and dandruff, and antimicrobials can help damaged skin. No dog owner should be without one of the dog shampoos that requires no water or rinsing. These are wonderful for puppies, spot-baths, and emergencies.

## Bathing

If you use your own tub for dog bathing, place a nonskid mat in the bottom of it and help your dog in and out so she doesn't slip. A hand-held sprayer is essential for indoor bathing. Remember to use water that you would be comfortable using for a shower. Warm water tends to open

the hair follicles and helps loosen dead hair. Keep one hand under the spray so you can monitor the water temperature.

Start by wetting down the dog to the skin, leaving the head for last. Be sure the water isn't just running off the top of the dog. You need to soak the undercoat down to the skin. Mix the shampoo with water first. Use a big sponge to apply it and then use your hands to work up a moderate lather. Rinsing is a crucial step; shampoo remaining in the coat can cause dryness and itchiness. Begin rinsing from the front and top of the dog and work rearwards. To keep your dog from shaking, keep one hand clenched around the base of one ear. Do not use a cream rinse.

## Drying

Don't let your dog outside on a chilly day when still wet from a bath. You have removed the oils from the coat and saturated your dog down to

*A clean, well-groomed Jack keeps your furniture cleaner and hair free (sort of).*

# Skin Problems

Skin problems make up most of the "non-well" cases a veterinarian sees every day. Problems can result from parasites, allergies, bacteria, fungus, endocrine disorders, and a long list of other possible causes.

### Dermatophytosis

Dermatophytosis, better known as ringworm, is one of the most common fungal disorders of dogs. In one study, JRT's were one of two breeds with a significantly higher proportion of ringworm cases. Puppies were especially predisposed to infection. Ringworm is contagious to other animals (including humans), so a dog with ringworm should be managed with this in mind. It can also be transmitted by contact with contaminated objects (such as combs) and in some cases, from soil in which the ringworm fungi reside.

The most common areas of infection are the head and forelimbs. The fungi invade the outermost layers of the skin, along with the nails and hair, causing an expanding area of hair loss with crusting, redness, and scaling around the margins. Diagnosis is by several means, including examination under a special (Wood's) light, microscopic examination, and culture. Often the disease will go away by itself after a few months, but treatment with antifungal medications is suggested. The environment should be thoroughly cleaned, including bleaching and steam cleaning where possible.

the skin, so it is far wetter than it would ever get by going swimming and thus more likely to become chilled. Vigorous towel drying will help dislodge any remaining dead hairs. Comb the hair when it is almost dry, and remove any new errant hairs that may have appeared during the process.

> ### ☆ JACK FACT ☆
>
> **Pyoderma**
> Pyoderma, with pus-filled bumps and crusting, is another common skin disease. Impetigo is characterized by such bumps and crusting most often in the groin area of puppies. Both are treated with antibiotics and antibacterial shampoos.

## Skin Allergies

Flea allergy dermatitis (FAD) is the most common of all skin problems. When even one flea bites a susceptible dog the flea's saliva causes an allergic reaction that results in intense itching, not only in the vicinity of the flea bite, but often all over the dog and especially on its rump, legs, and paws. The dog chews these areas and causes irritation leading to crusted bumps.

Besides FAD, dogs can have allergic reactions to pollens or other inhaled allergens. Whereas human inhalant allergies usually result in respiratory symptoms, canine inhalant allergies usually result in itchy skin. The condition typically first appears in young dogs and gets progressively worse. The main sites of itching seem to be the face, ears, feet, forelegs, armpits, and abdomen. The dog rubs and chews these areas, traumatizing the skin and leading to secondary bacterial infections. Because the feet are so often affected, many people erroneously assume the dog is allergic to grass or dew. Although such contact allergies do exist, they are far less common than flea, inhalant, or food allergies.

Dogs can also have food allergies that cause itching. They are discussed on page 45.

Allergens can be isolated with an intradermal skin test, in which small amounts of various allergen extracts are injected under the skin. The skin is then monitored for localized allergic reactions. Blood tests are also available and are less expensive, but they are not as comprehensive as skin testing. Either test should be performed by a veterinarian with training in the field of allergic skin diseases, as the results can be difficult to interpret.

## Hot Spots

A reddened moist itchy spot that suddenly appears is most likely a "hot spot" (pyotraumatic dermatitis), which arises from an itch-scratch-chew cycle resulting most commonly from fleas or allergies. Wash the area with an oatmeal-based shampoo, and prevent the dog from further chewing. If possible, shave the area first. Several home remedies have

---

### ☆ JACK FACT ☆

**Fleas and Tapeworms**

Tapeworms look like moving white flat worms when fresh, or like rice grains (usually around the dog's anus) when dried out. Although they are one of the least debilitating of all the worms, their segments can produce anal itching. Because tapeworms are in the cestode family, they are not affected by the same kinds of dewormers and preventives as the other common worms, which are in the nematode family. The only preventive is to diligently rid your JRT of fleas, because fleas transmit the most common tapeworm (Dipylidium) to dogs. Another type of tapeworm (Taenia) can be obtained from eating infected wild animals.

been suggested, including the application of Listerine or Gold Bond powder, but these do not always work and severe cases should receive veterinary attention. Your veterinarian can also prescribe anti-inflammatory medication and, if needed, antibiotics. As a temporary measure, you can give an allergy pill (ask your veterinarian about dosage), which alleviates some itching and causes drowsiness, both of which should decrease chewing.

# External Parasites

Parasites remain one of the most common causes of skin and coat problems in dogs. However, their damage is more than skin deep; many external parasites also carry

*It's a jungle out there...*

serious, even deadly, systemic diseases.

## Fleas

Fleas have long been the bane of dogs, but recent advances have finally put dog owners on the winning side in the fight against fleas. In any but the mildest of infestations, the new products available are well worth their initial higher purchase price. It's a lot cheaper to put an expensive product on your dog once every three months than to reapply a cheap one every day.

Always read the ingredients. You may think you're getting a deal with a less expensive product that is applied the same and boasts of the same results as one of the more expensive products, but you're not getting a deal if it doesn't contain the right ingredients. Some of the major ingredients in the newer products are
• imidacloprid (for example, Advantage), a liquid applied once a month on the animal's back. It gradually distributes itself over the entire skin surface and kills at least 98 percent of the fleas on the animal within 24 hours and will continue to kill fleas for a month. It can withstand water, but not repeated swimming or bathing.
• fipronil (for example, Frontline), which comes as either a spray that you must apply all over the dog's body or as a self-distributing liquid applied only on the dog's back. Once applied, fipronil collects in the hair follicles and then wicks out over time. Thus, it is resistant to being

washed off and can kill fleas for up to three months on dogs. It is also effective on ticks for a shorter period.

• lufenuron (for example, Program), which is given as a pill once a month. Fleas that bite the dog and ingest the lufenuron in the dog's system are rendered sterile. It is extremely safe. All animals in the environment must be treated in order for the regime to be effective, however.

Traditional flea control products are either less effective or less safe than these newer products. The permethrins and pyrethrins are safe, but have virtually no residual action. The large family of cholinesterase inhibitors (Dursban, Diazinon, malathion, Sevin, Carbaryl, Pro-Spot, Spotton) last a little longer, but have been known to kill dogs when overused, when used in combination with cholinesterase inhibiting yard products, or with cholinesterase inhibiting dewormers. Ultrasonic flea repelling collars have been shown to be both ineffective on fleas and irritating to dogs. Feeding dogs brewer's yeast or garlic will not get rid of fleas.

## Ticks

Two newer products for tick control are amitraz collars (tick collars) and fipronil spray or liquid. Neither will keep ticks totally off your dog, but they may discourage them from staying or implanting. Even with these precautions you should still use your hands to feel for ticks in your dogs whenever you are in a potential tick infested area.

---

## ☆ JACK FACT ☆

**Ticks and Ehrlichiosis**

Ehrlichiosis is an under-diagnosed yet potentially fatal disease spread by ticks that parasitizes white blood cells and cripples the immune system. Symptoms may include lack of energy, dullness of coat, occasional vomiting, occasional loss of appetite, coughing, arthritis, muscle wasting, seizures, spontaneous bleeding, anemia, or a host of other nonspecific signs. Aside from a fever in the initial phases of the disease, dogs may not exhibit definite signs of illness—they may just not seem "quite right." Definitive diagnosis is made by getting a blood titre and testing for all strains of ehrlichia. It can be treated effectively if caught early.

---

Ticks can be found anywhere on the dog, but most often burrow around the ears, neck, chest, and between the toes. To remove a tick, use a tissue or tweezers, because some diseases can be transmitted to humans. Grasp the tick as close to the skin as possible, and pull slowly and steadily, trying not to leave the head in the dog. Don't squeeze the tick, as this can inject its contents into the dog. Clean the site with alcohol. Often a bump will remain after the tick is removed, even if you got the head. It will go away with time.

Ticks carry many serious diseases, including ehrlichiosis, Rocky

Mountain spotted fever, babesiosis, and Lyme disease.

## Mites

Mites are tiny organisms that are in the tick and spider family. Chemicals that are effective on fleas have no effect on mites. Of the many types of mites, only a few typically cause problems in dogs.

**Sarcoptes mange:** Sarcoptes mites cause sarcoptic mange, which causes intense itching, often characterized by scaling of the ear tips, and small bumps and crusts of other affected areas. Most of the lesions are found on the ear tips, abdomen, elbows, and hocks. Treatment requires repeated shampoos or dips

*Healthy skin and ears often go together.*

of not only the affected dog, but other household pets that are in contact with the infected dog. It is highly contagious, even to humans, and spread by direct contact. Skin scrapings may reveal the responsible *Sarcoptes scabiei* mite. The presence of just one mite lends a definite diagnosis, but the absence of mites doesn't mean they aren't present.

**Demodex mange:** Demodex mites cause demodectic mange. Unlike sarcoptic mange, it is not contagious and is not usually itchy. Most cases of demodectic mange appear in puppies, and most consist of only a few patches that often go away by themselves. This localized variety is not considered hereditary. In some cases it begins as a diffuse moth-eaten appearance, particularly around the lips and eyes, or on the front legs, or the dog has many localized spots. These cases tend to get worse until the dog has generalized demodectic mange. Demodectic mange affecting the feet is also common, and can be extremely resistant to treatment. Aggressive treatment using repeated amitraz insecticidal dips is needed for generalized demodicosis, but is not suggested for localized. The hair should be clipped to allow the dips to penetrate to the skin more easily. Benzoyl peroxide shampoos have a follicular flushing action and should be used for both localized and generalized forms. A definite diagnosis with a skin scraping should be performed before beginning treatment and before ending it. Because the

*Demodex canis* mite is thought to be a normal inhabitant of the dog's hair follicles, the presence of an occasional mite is not normally sufficient evidence to diagnose a dog with demodectic mange.

**Cheyletialla:** Cheyletialla mites are contagious and cause mild itchiness. They look like small white specks in the dog's hair near the skin. Many flea insecticides also kill these mites, but they are better treated by using special shampoos or dips.

Sarcoptic, demodectic, and cheyletialla mites have all been successfully eradicated with injections of ivermectin. This treatment is considered "off-label" and should only be performed by a veterinarian in serious cases.

**Ear mites:** A dog with ear mites will scratch its ears, shake its head, and perhaps hold its head sideways. The ear mite's signature is a dark, dry, waxy buildup resembling coffee grounds in the ear canal, usually of both ears. Sometimes the tiny mites can be seen with a magnifying glass if the material is placed on a dark background.

---

### ☆ JACK FACT ☆

**Prick Ears**
Some Jacks have ears that stick straight up, which is faulty according to most standards. If the dog is still young and the ears somewhat pliable, they may be able to be coaxed into tipping forward by taping them. Otherwise, enjoy them!

---

Separate a dog with ear mites from other pets and wash your hands after handling its ears. Ideally, every pet in a household should be treated. Your veterinarian can provide the best medication. Because ear mites are also found in the dog's fur all over its body, you should also treat the dog's fur with a pyrethrin-based shampoo or spray.

# Ear Care

Unlike in humans, the dog's ear canal is made up of an initial long vertical segment that then abruptly angles to run horizontally toward the skull. This configuration provides a moist environment in which various ear infections can flourish. Check your dog's ears regularly and don't allow moisture or debris to accumulate in them.

### Ear-ly Warnings

Ear problems can be difficult to cure once they have become established, so that early veterinary attention is crucial. Signs of ear problems include inflammation, discharge, debris, foul odor, pain, scratching, shaking, tilting of the head, or circling to one side. Bacterial and yeast infections, ear mites or ticks, foreign bodies, inhalant allergies, seborrhea, or hypothyroidism are possible underlying problems. Because the ear canal is lined with skin, any skin disorder that affects the dog elsewhere can also strike its ears. Foxtails (see page 140) are a common cause of ear problems in dogs that spend time outdoors. Keep the ear lubricated with mineral oil and seek veterinary treatment as soon as possible.

If your dog has ear debris but no signs of discomfort or itching, you can try cleaning the ear yourself, but be forewarned that overzealous cleaning can irritate the skin lining the ear canal. You can buy products to clean the ear or use a homemade mixture of one part alcohol to two parts white vinegar. Hold the ear near its base and quickly squeeze in the ear cleaner (the slower it drips the more it will tickle). Gently massage the liquid downward and squish it all around. Then stand back and let your dog shake it all out (be sure you're outdoors). If the ear has so much debris that repeated rinses

don't clean it right up, you have a problem that will need veterinary attention. If the ear is red, swollen, or painful do not attempt to clean it yourself. Your dog may need to be sedated for cleaning and may have a serious problem. Cleaning solutions will flush debris but will not kill mites or cure infections. Don't stick cotton swabs down in the ear canal, as they can irritate the skin and pack debris into the horizontal canal. Don't use powders in the ear, which can cake, or hydrogen peroxide, which can leave the ear moist.

## Nail Care

Jack Russell nails evolved to withstand strenuous running and digging.

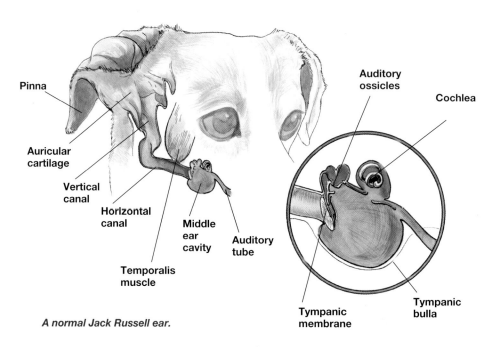

Pinna

Auricular cartilage

Vertical canal

Horizontal canal

Middle ear cavity

Auditory tube

Temporalis muscle

Auditory ossicles

Cochlea

Tympanic membrane

Tympanic bulla

*A normal Jack Russell ear.*

*Even puppies need nail care.*

Unless your Jack is a marathon runner or digger, you're going to need to trim her nails regularly. The most common problem associated with overly long nails happens when the nail becomes snagged on a tree root or even carpet loop, pulling the nail from its bed or dislocating the toe. In addition, overly long nails impact on the ground with every step, causing discomfort and eventually splayed feet and lameness. If dew claws (the rudimentary "thumbs" on the wrists) are left untrimmed they can get caught on things more easily and can be ripped out or actually loop around and grow into the dog's leg. You must prevent this by trimming your dog's nails every week or two.

### Trimming

It's easier to cut the nails by holding the foot backwards, much as a horse's hoof is held when being shod. This way your JRT can't see what's going on, and you can see the bottom of the nail. Here you will see a solid core culminating in a hollowed nail. Cut the tip up to the core, but not beyond. On occasion you will slip up and cause the nail to bleed. Apply styptic powder to the nail to stop the bleeding. If this is not available dip the nail in flour or hold it to a wet tea bag. And be more careful next time!

# Eye Care

Eye care should never be approached with a "wait and see" attitude. Take note of squinting, redness, itching, tearing, dullness, mucus discharge, or any change in pupil size or reactivity. Look for evidence of a luxated (displaced) lens, which might include part of the lens edge becoming visible through the pupil, or even emerging through the pupil into the front portion of the eye. Any time your dog's pupils do not react to light or when one eye reacts differently from another, take it to the veterinarian immediately. It could indicate a serious ocular or neurological problem.

Squinting or tearing can be due to an irritated cornea or foreign body. Examine under the lids and flood the eye with saline solution, or use a moist cotton swab to remove any debris. A watery discharge without squinting can be a symptom of allergies or a tear drainage problem. A clogged tear drainage duct can cause the tears to drain onto the face rather than the normal drainage through the nose. Your veterinarian can diagnose a drainage problem with a simple test.

A thick mucus discharge usually indicates a more serious problem, including conjunctivitis, lid irritation, or "dry eye" *(keratoconjunctivitis sicca)*. These conditions should be treated by your veterinarian.

As your JRT ages it is natural that the lens of the eye becomes a little hazy. You will notice this as a slightly grayish appearance behind the pupils. But if this occurs at a young age, or if the lens looks white or opaque, ask your veterinarian to check your dog for cataracts. In cataracts the lens becomes so opaque that light can no longer reach the retina; as in humans, the lens can be surgically replaced with an artificial lens.

# Dental Care

Between four and seven months of age, JRT puppies will begin to shed their baby teeth and show off new permanent teeth. Often deciduous (baby) teeth, especially the canines (fangs), are not shed, so that the permanent tooth grows in beside the baby tooth. If this condition persists after the permanent teeth are fully in, consult your veterinarian. Retained baby teeth can cause misalignment of adult teeth. Correct occlusion is important for good dental health. In a correct JRT bite, the top incisors should fit snugly in front of the bottom incisors, with the top canines just behind the bottom canines. If the bottom canines are behind or opposed to the top canines, the bottom ones can be displaced inward and pierce the palate.

## Plaque and Tartar

Tooth plaque and tartar are not only unsightly, but contribute to bad breath and health problems. If not removed, plaque will attract bacteria and minerals, which will harden into tartar. Plaque can cause infections to form along the gum line, then spread rootward causing irreversible periodontal disease with tissue, bone, and tooth loss. The bacteria may also sometimes enter the bloodstream and cause infection in the kidneys and heart valves.

Dry food and hard dog biscuits, carrots, rawhide and dental chewies

*Examination and care of the teeth are vital for good health.*

are only minimally helpful at removing plaque. Prescription dog food is available that will decrease tartar accumulation, but brushing your JRT's teeth (optimally daily) with a dog toothpaste and brush is the best plaque remover. Most dogs are surprisingly cooperative. Your dog's teeth may have to be cleaned under anesthesia as often as once a year if you do not brush them.

*A well-groomed JRT feels better, looks better, and has a head start on a long and healthy life. You wouldn't want any less for him—even if he would rather be covered with dirt!*

---

### ☆ JACK FACT ☆

**Tooth Injuries**

Tough terriers can injure their teeth many ways, but one way they often do so is when their owners show off their tenacious grips by allowing their dogs to hang on to and swing from sticks. This may seem like fun, but it's not worth the veterinary bills and pain that can ultimately arise from loosened, cracked, and worn teeth.

# Chapter Six

# Dr. Jackyll and Mr. Hyde

When the world beckons with holes that need digging, clothes that need shredding, shoes that need chewing, cats that need chasing, trails that need following, and so many, many things that need barking at, what's a poor Jack to do? What's a poor Jack owner to do? Even good Jacks, with good owners, do bad things. The real test of a good owner is how you deal with these situations. Until recently even the best owners had little choice of where to turn for advice for dog behavior problems. Well meaning but misguided training advice from friends, breeders, or even veterinarians or dog trainers without a scientific background in dog behavior too often only made things worse. Far too many Jack Russells have been relinquished because their owners simply never were given the proper advice to deal with their dog's behavioral problems. Great strides have been made in recent years in canine behavioral therapy. Qualified behaviorists will consider both behavioral and medical therapies. As a first step in any serious behavior problem, a thorough veterinary exam should be performed.

*The face of innocence?*

## Behavior Changes

When a normally active, impetuous Jack suddenly slows down for no apparent reason, it's worth investigating. Lethargy is the most common behavioral sign of disease. Possible causes include:
• infection (check for fever)
• anemia (check gum color)
• circulatory problem (check gum color and pulse)
• pain (check limbs, neck, and vertebrae for signs of discomfort upon movement; check mouth, ears, and eyes for signs of pain; check abdomen for pain—pain in the abdomen often cause dogs to stand in a hunched position)
• sudden loss of vision

---

### ☆ JACK FACT ☆

**Punishment**
Harsh or repeated punishment never helps teach your dog anything except to fear you. If punishment doesn't work the first time, why would it work the second, third, or fourth time? Instead, concentrate on rewarding desirable behavior.

---

*And these three little puppies went "wee, wee" all over the home—unless they are supervised at all times.*

• poisoning (check gum color, pupil reaction, look for signs of vomiting or abdominal pain)
• cancer
• metabolic diseases

Unprecedented behavior of any kind, but particularly persistent circling or pacing, disorientation, loss of balance, head-pressing, hiding, tremors, seizures, lack of bowel or urine control, or dramatic change in appetite are usually signs of a physical problem and need to be checked by your veterinarian.

# Housebreaking Woes

It takes a while for your pup to realize where he can and can't use the bathroom. With some concerted effort you can speed the process along, but don't expect miracles in baby puppies. Follow these rules for saving your carpets and creating a housebroken puppy:

**Restrict your pup's unsupervised freedom in the house:** All canines have a natural desire to avoid soiling their denning area. The problem is your pup only considers his own bed to be the equivalent of the den, and so he walks a few feet away and eliminates in the middle of your room. By restricting your puppy to a wolf den sized area, such as a cage, when you cannot supervise him you will eliminate this elimination problem.

**Don't let accidents happen:** When your puppy has to go he has to go right now! Puppies have very weak control over their bladder and bowels, so if you don't take them to their doggy outhouse often and immediately, they may not be able to avoid soiling. When a pup soils in the house, he labels that area as his bathroom and is likely to go there again. If your pup does have an accident indoors, clean and deodorize the spot thoroughly and block the pup's access to that area.

Learn to predict when your puppy will have to relieve himself:

• Immediately after awakening, and soon after heavy drinking or playing, your puppy will urinate.

• Right after eating, or if nervous, your puppy will have to defecate.

• Car rides also tend to elicit defecation—even in the car.

• Circling, whining, sniffing, and generally acting worried usually signals that defecation is imminent.

**Know your puppy's limits:** Don't expect more from your pup than he is physically able to give. A rule of thumb is that a puppy can, at most, hold his bowels for as many hours as the pup is months old. If the pup is forced to stay confined longer than his limit, you are causing an accident and teaching your pup to go in the wrong place.

**Punishment doesn't help:** Dog owners have been rubbing their dogs' noses in their mess for years, and it hasn't been working for years. Dog owners, unfortunately, are slow learners. The dogs trained this way appear to learn just as slowly. Punishing a dog for a mess it has made earlier is totally fruitless; it only succeeds in convincing the dog that every once in a while, for no apparent reason, you are apt to go insane and attack. It is a perfect recipe for ruining a trusting relationship. That guilty look you may think your dog is exhibiting is really a look of fear that you have once again lost your mind. Even if you catch your dog in the act, overly enthusiastic correction only teaches the dog not to relieve himself in your presence, even when outside. This doesn't mean you ignore him as he ruins your carpet. You can yell "No! Out!" and hustle him outside, and then reward his going outside, as long as you catch him in the act.

**Reward correct behavior:** When the puppy does relieve himself outdoors, heap on the praise and let him know how pleased you are. Adding a food treat really gets the point across.

**Go outside:** Most owners think they've done their part by opening the door and pushing the pup outside, but chances are the pup spent his time outside trying to get back inside to his owner. Puppies do not like to be alone, and knowing you are on the other side of the door makes the outdoors unappealing. So you must go outside with the pup every time, and be ready to reward him for his good deed.

## Adult Soiling

No matter how gifted your Jack is, he will probably not be reliably housebroken until he is an adult. If an adult continues to eliminate in the

**The Cage or Crate**
A cage provides a snug, secure place for your Jack to get away from it all, and for you to keep your Jack out of trouble when you're not home. Place your dog in the cage when he is sleepy; a chewbone can also help him enjoy the experience. Work up to longer times gradually, and never use the cage as a place of punishment.

house, or if a formerly housebroken dog begins to soil, a veterinary examination is warranted. You and your veterinarian will need to consider the following possibilities:

• Older dogs may simply not have the bladder control that they had as youngsters; a doggy door is the best solution.

• Older spayed females may dribble urine, especially when sleeping; ask your veterinarian about drug therapies.

*TERRIER-IFIC!*
Moose's first two families had to give up on him. He was into everything, destructive, and just plain incorrigible. His last chance came from someone who saw a dog in need of a job in life. She adopted him, put his mind to work, and created a wonderfully behaved house dog—and also one of the most famous JRT's in the world—known better as "Eddie" on the TV series *Frasier.*

• Frequent urination of small amounts (especially if the urine is bloody or dark) may indicate an infection of the urinary tract. Such infections must be treated promptly.

• Increased urine production can be a sign of kidney disease or diabetes; your veterinarian can test for and treat these disorders. Never restrict water from these dogs; a doggy door is a better way to cope.

• Sometimes a housebroken dog will be forced to soil the house because of a bout of diarrhea, and afterwards will continue to soil in the same area. If this happens restrict that area from the dog, deodorize the area with an enzymatic cleaner, and revert to basic housebreaking lessons.

• Male dogs may "lift their leg" inside of the house as a means of marking it as theirs. Castration will often solve this problem as long as it is performed before the habit has become established; otherwise diligent deodorizing and the use of some dog deterring odorants (available at pet stores) may help.

• Submissive dogs, especially young females, may urinate upon greeting you; punishment only makes this "submissive urination" worse. For these dogs, be careful not to bend over or otherwise dominate them. Keep greetings calm. Submissive urination is usually outgrown as the dog gains more confidence.

Some dogs defecate or urinate due to the stress of separation anxiety; you must treat the anxiety to cure the symptom. Dogs that mess their cage when left in it are usually suffering from separation anxiety or anxiety about being closed in a cage. Other telltale signs of anxiety-produced elimination are drooling, scratching, and escape oriented behavior. You need to treat separation anxiety and start cage training over, placing the dog in it for a short period of time and working up gradually to longer times. Dogs that suffer from cage claustrophobia but not separation anxiety do better if left loose in a dog-proofed room or yard.

# Home Destruction

One of the joys of dog ownership is that no matter what you've done, the one family member you can count on being overwhelmed with joy at your return home is your dog. The joyous reunion is greatly diminished, however, if you are over-whelmed by the sight of your vandalized home. The vandal is your loving dog, telling you how much he loves you as only a dog can do.

But before we get to how your dog destroying your home is a token of his love for you, let's talk about the times in which it isn't. Puppies are natural demolition dogs, and they vandalize for the sheer ecstasy that only a search and destroy mission can provide. The best cure (besides old age) is supervision and prevention.

## Boredom

Adult Jacks are still puppies at heart and may destroy items through frustration or boredom. The best way to deal with these dogs is to tire them with both physical and mental exercise an hour or so before leaving your dog. Several toys are available that can provide hours of entertainment;

*Jack Russell Terriers aren't really destructive; they just like to create modern art with their teeth.*

*Jack Russell Terriers don't like being left home alone.*

for example, some can be filled with peanut butter or treats in such a way that it takes the dog a very long time to extract the food from the toy. Puppies have a need to chew. Give them an assortment of chew toys to satisfy the urge.

### Anxiety

When calm adult JRT's destroy your home, it could be because they are upset at being left. They are not destroying out of spite, as is too often assumed, but out of anxiety. Being left alone is an extremely stressful situation for these highly social animals. They react by becoming agitated and trying to escape from confinement. Perhaps they reason that if they can just get out of the house they will be reunited with their people. The telltale signature of a dog suffering from this *separation anxiety* is that most of their destructive behavior is focused on doors and windows. Punishing these dogs is ineffective because it actually increases the anxiety level of the dog, as it comes to both look forward to and dread the owner's return.

**The cage may not be a cure:** Keeping the dog in its cage may save your home, but seldom deals with the problem. Some dogs become so anxious at being placed in the cage that they need to undergo behavior modification every bit as much as dogs that are allowed the run of the house. Such dogs often urinate or defecate in their cage, rip up bedding, dig and bite at the cage door, bark, pant, shake, and drool.

**Treating separation anxiety:**
Separation anxiety should be treated like any other fear, that is, by working slowly. This is done by leaving the dog alone for very short periods of time and gradually working to longer periods, taking care to never allow the dog to become anxious during any session. When you *must* leave your dog for long periods during the conditioning program, leave him in a different part of the house than the one in which the conditioning sessions take place. This way you won't undo all of your work if he becomes overstressed by your long absence.

When you return home, no matter how horrified or relieved you are at the condition of the house, greet your dog calmly. Then have him perform a simple trick or obedience exercise so that you have an excuse to praise him. In severe cases your veterinarian can prescribe antianxiety medications to help your pet deal with being left alone. These medications are most useful when combined with the gradual desensitization techniques outlined previously. It takes a lot of patience, and often a whole lot of self-control, but it's not fair to you or your dog to let this situation continue. It will only get worse.

# Unruly Behavior

If you can't handle a little unruly behavior, don't get a Jack Russell Terrier! One of the traits that attracts people to Jack Russells in the first place is their high energy level; yet it's also one of the main reasons cited for giving them up. This high energy was needed in order to sustain a hunting terrier through a long, arduous hunt. You can't blame your Jack for acting how he was bred to act. Nonetheless, that doesn't mean you should allow a little wild dog to wreak havoc in your home. You can take several measures to direct your Jack's activity toward good, rather than evil, if you take the time. First you have to define the nature of your dog's misbehavior.

## Hyperactivity

Jack Russell Terriers were initially developed for their ability to spend a long, strenuous day running with the hounds and bolting quarry. This means throwing a ball for ten minutes is not going to tire your Jack.

*Toys are a great way to save your valuable belongings.*

These are energetic, inquisitive dogs. If your dog is driving you crazy it's probably because he's going crazy through lack of stimulation. The best cure for an overactive Jack is lots of mental and physical exercise. This means a good run, a fast paced game, or a challenging obedience lesson several times a day. A dog agility course is a great mind and body exerciser.

### Jumping Up

Jumping up to greet you is a normal canine behavior, but it can be an irritating or dangerous one. Teach your dog to sit and stay so that you can kneel down to his level for greetings. When he does jump up, simply say *"No"* and step backward, so that his paws meet only air. Teaching your dog a special command (such as "jump up") that lets him know it's OK to jump up can actually help him discriminate the difference.

Some Jacks are so excited when guests arrive that they jump all over them, which is not always appreciated. If your guests include very small children, you're usually best to keep the dog away, but if you always lock the dog away whenever any guest arrives he will only get more crazed to greet people and be out of control when he finally gets the chance. The more people he gets a chance to greet politely, the less excited he'll be about meeting new people, and the less inclined to jump on them. This requires having friends that will work with you by kneeling and greeting your sitting Jack, and not allowing him to jump on them. Your Jack should learn that polite dogs are greeted by guests, but impolite dogs are not. After greeting, have a special chew treat or toy for your Jack to entertain himself with in the same room, so he learns to be part of the group without going crazy.

### Barking

Barking is one of the Jack Russell's natural tools that helped to bolt foxes during a hunt. It is also a life-saving trait that helps to locate a dog that is stuck underground and must be dug out. Don't begrudge your Jack's barking; it's part of his heritage. That doesn't mean you should live with nonstop barking, however. Barking while hunting or playing or at suspicious happenings around the home are perfectly acceptable behaviors for most circumstances. Barking at falling leaves is not.

If your dog won't stop barking when you tell him to, distract him with a loud noise of your own. Begin to anticipate when your dog will start barking, distract him, and reward him for quiet behavior. You will actually create a better watchdog by discouraging your dog from barking at non-threatening objects and encouraging him to bark at suspicious people. Allow your Jack to bark momentarily at strangers, and then call him to you and praise him for quiet behavior, distracting him with an obedience exercise if need be.

A dog stuck in a pen in the backyard will bark. What else is there to do? Isolated dogs will often bark through frustration or as a means of getting attention and alleviating loneliness. Even if the attention gained includes punishment, they continue to bark in order to obtain the temporary presence of the owner. The fault is not theirs; they should never have been banned to solitary confinement in the first place.

The simplest solution is to move the dog's quarters to a less isolated location. Let the dog in your house or fence in your entire yard. If barking occurs when you put your dog to bed, move his bed into your bedroom, or condition your dog by rewarding him for successively longer periods of quiet behavior. The distraction of a special chew toy, given only at bedtime, may help alleviate barking. Remember, a sleeping dog can't bark, so exercise can be a big help.

For stubborn barkers, a citronella collar is sometimes effective. These collars spray a squirt of citronella (which dogs don't like) whenever the dog barks. They are more effective and safer than bark activated shock collars. If your dog's barking is so bad that you are considering placing him because of the neighbor's complaints, talk to your veterinarian about the pros and cons of surgical debarking as a last ditch effort.

## Escaping

Jack Russells are smart dogs— some would call them evil geniuses. Combine this with their innate ability to squeeze through narrow passages and go underground and you have

*Some escapes are just too easy...*

the perfect escape artist. Too often, however, their owners inadvertently hone their Houdini talents by making escape relatively easy in the first place. The best way to teach a dog to do something is to start simple and work up. By the same reasoning, the best way to inadvertently teach a dog to escape from your yard would be to start with a weak fence and then try to start fixing it little by little. Teach your dog from the start that there is no escaping your maximum security yard, and that all efforts are futile!

## Digging

If you have visions of restoring your lawn to the lush green carpet you had before your Jack moved in, forget it. Jack Russell Terriers are natural born diggers. The best you can do is to provide your Jack an acceptable place to dig, and direct him to it whenever he begins digging in an off-limits area.

# Fearfulness

Even the bravest of Jack Russells can sometimes develop illogical fears, or phobias. The most common are fears of strange people or dogs, gunshots, or thunder. Every once in a while a particularly imaginative Jack will come up with a bizarre fear all its own, but it can usually be treated using the same general concepts.

The cardinal rule of working with a fearful dog is to never push it into situations that might overwhelm it. Some people erroneously think the best way to deal with a scared dog is to inundate him with the very thing he's afraid of, until he gets used to it.

This concept (called flooding) doesn't work because the dog is usually so terrified he never gets over his fear enough to realize the situation is safe.

Other owners tend to try to reassure their Jack by petting or holding him when scared. This only reinforces the behavior, and often also convinces the dog that the owner is frightened as well. You want to maintain a jolly attitude and make your dog work for praise. The first step is to teach your dog a few simple commands; performing these exercises correctly gives you a reason to praise him and also increases his sense of security because he knows what's expected of him.

In some cases, the dog is petrified at even the lowest level of exposure to whatever he is scared of. You may have to use antianxiety drugs in conjunction with training to calm your dog enough to make progress. This is when you need the advice of a behaviorist.

## Shyness

If the dog is afraid of people, don't let people push themselves on him. This frightens the dog, sometimes to the extent that a person could be bitten. Shy dogs are like shy people in some ways: They are not so much afraid of people as they are of being the center of attention of people. Strangers should be asked to ignore shy dogs, even when approached by the dog. When the dog gets braver, have the stranger offer him a tidbit, at first while not even looking at the dog. It's not necessary for your dog to love strangers, but he should be comfortable enough with them so that he can be treated by a veterinarian, boarded, or caught if lost, without being emotionally traumatized.

## Noise Phobias

Fear of thunder or gunshots are common problems in older dogs. To see a normally happy-go-lucky Jack quivering and panting in the closet at the slight rumblings of a distant thunderstorm is a sad sight, and it only gets worse with time. Do something about it at the first sign of trouble. Try to avoid fostering these fears. Act cheerful when a thunderstorm strikes, and play with your dog or give it a tidbit. Once a dog develops a noise phobia, try to find a recording of that noise. Play it at a very low level and reward your dog for calm behavior. Gradually increase the intensity and duration of the recording. A program of gradual desensitization, with the dog exposed to the frightening person or thing and then rewarded for calm behavior, is time-consuming but is the best way to alleviate any fear. Again, calming drugs may be helpful during training but should not become a crutch.

# Aggression

Many types of aggression can occur in dogs, and the treatment for them can be very different. Jacks are naturally boisterous and playful dogs, and they don't tend to back

down from a perceived challenge. Often new Jack Russell owners have difficulty telling if their dog is actually behaving aggressively.

## Is It Really Aggression?

Puppies and dogs play by growling and biting. Usually they play with their littermates this way, but if yours is an only puppy, you will just have to make do. So many people have seen horror stories about dogs that when their pup growls and bites they immediately label it as a problem biter. You need to know the difference between true aggression and playful aggression. Look for these clues that tell you it's all in good fun:
• wagging tail
• down on elbows in front, with the rump in the air (the play-bow position)
• barks intermingled with growls
• lying down or rolling over
• bounding leaps or running in circles
• mouthing or chewing on you or other objects

On the other hand, look for these clues to identify aggression:
• low growl combined with a direct stare

- tail held stiffly
- sudden, unpredictable bites
- growling or biting in defense of food, toys, or bed
- growling or biting in response to punishment

Chances are your Jack is simply playing. Still, this doesn't mean you should let him use you as a chew-stick. When your pup bites you, simply say *"Ouch! No!"* and remove your chomped hand (or other part) from his mouth. Replace it with a toy. Hitting your dog is uncalled for—he was just trying to play and meant no harm. Hitting is also a form of aggression that could give your dog the idea that he had better try (bite) harder next time because you're playing the game a lot rougher. You don't want to encourage playful aggression but you don't want to punish it. You want to redirect it.

*Most Jacks live in harmony with their special people.*

## Aggression Toward Other Dogs

If your dog is really acting aggressively rather than playfully, you need to decide if your dog's aggression is directed toward other dogs and animals or toward people. Aggression toward other animals does not mean a dog will be aggressive toward people.

Aggression toward strange dogs is a biologically normal trait of canines, but one that is not suitable for dogs in today's world. Many Jack Russells are naturally dog-aggressive, and you may never be able to trust them around other dogs. You can try to shape your dog to be as tolerant as possible, however. It's natural for your dog to defend his home territory against strange dogs. The problem develops when you try to introduce a new dog into the home, or when your dog thinks the world is his personal territory. Because male dogs mark their territory by urinating on various posts, the more you allow a dog to mark the more likely that dog will behave aggressively toward other dogs in that area. When introducing new dogs, it usually works best if the dogs meet on neutral territory and have a mutual distraction. Going for a long walk together in a new area, with each dog held on leash, is an ideal way for dogs to get used to one another and associate the other with a pleasurable event. Many people who hunt with their dogs find that Jacks that hunt together are too involved with working together to have any desire to fight.

*Many—but not all—Jack Russells get along well with other dogs.*

Many Jack Russell housemates just don't see eye to eye. Problems between housemates are most likely to occur between dogs of the same sex and same age. Seniority counts for a lot in the dog world, and a young pup will usually grow up respecting its elders. Sometimes, a youngster gets aspirations to be top dog, however, or two dogs of about the same age never quite decide which one is leadership material. Then the trouble starts. Remember to first decide if this is natural rough play behavior between the two. An occasional disagreement, too, is normal. A disagreement that draws blood or leaves one dog screaming or in which the two dogs cannot be separated is a potential problem.

Repeated disagreements spell trouble. Neutering one or both males in a two male dominance battle can sometimes help, but neutering females seldom helps.

It's human nature to soothe the underdog and punish the bully, but you'd be doing the underdog the

---

### ☆ **JACK FACT** ☆

**Don't Look into My Eyes**
Unlike in humans, where direct eye contact is seen as a sign of sincerity, staring a dog directly in the eye is interpreted by the dog as a threat. It can cause a fearful or dominant dog to bite. Teach children not to stare at a strange dog.

worst favor you could. If your dogs are fighting for dominance, they are doing so in part because in the dog world, the dominant dog gets the lion's share of the most precious resources. You, and your attention, is the very most precious resource your dog can have. If you now give your attention to the loser, the winner will only try harder to beat the daylights out of the loser so your attention will go where it should go—to the winner. You will do your losing dog the best favor if you treat the winning dog like a king, and the losing dog like a prince. This means you always

*Don't confuse normal signs of playfulness and confidence with aggression.*

greet, pet, and feed the top dog first. It goes against human nature, but it goes with dog nature.

## Aggression Toward Humans

Much has been made of dominance problems in dogs; they probably occur less often than is thought, but when they do occur, the results can be aggression toward family members—with tragic consequences. Aggression toward humans is uncommon in Jacks. When it does happen, the best advice is to seek advice from a dog behaviorist. Remember, dominance aggression does not refer to the occasional nip in play or even disobedience. It is a serious situation in which the dog actively challenges and bites, or threatens to bite, a member of the family. Because it is a serious situation, it calls for serious treatment that is uncalled for in other cases.

**Signs of dominance aggression:** Dominance aggression most often occurs as a result of competition over a resource (such as trying to remove food or a toy, encroaching on the dog's sleeping quarters, or trying to step past the dog in a narrow hall), or during a perceived display of dominance by the owner (such as petting, grooming, scolding, or leading). Dogs may act more aggressively toward family members than strangers, and treat the family members in a dominant way, such as walking stiffly, staring, standing over them, and ignoring commands. Punishment usually only elicits further aggression.

Dominance aggression is more common in males than females, and occasionally (but not always) castration can help. Your veterinarian can give your intact (un-neutered) male dog a drug that will temporarily cause his hormonal state to be that of a neutered dog as a test to see if castration might help. Spaying a female will not help (and may even hinder) curing dominance aggression.

Owners of such dogs inevitably feel guilty and wonder "Where did I go wrong?" The fault is not entirely theirs. Although some actions of the owner may have helped create the problem, these same actions would not have produced dominance aggression in dogs that were not already predisposed to the problem. In predisposed dogs, owners who act in ways to foster the dog's opinion of himself as king can lead to problems. What would convince a dog that he ranked over a person? Actions such as:

• petting the dog on demand
• feeding the dog before eating your own meal
• allowing the dog to go first through doorways
• allowing the dog to win at games
• allowing the dog to have his way when he acts aggressively
• fearing the dog
• not punishing the dog for initial instances of aggression

## Dealing with Aggression

Treatment consists of putting the dog in his place, without direct confrontations. A popular training method from several years ago was the "alpha roll," in which you roll the dominant dog over on his back into a submissive position. However, this is a good way to get bitten, and most canine behaviorists now think it is a bad idea.

It's best to avoid situations that might lead to a showdown. If, however, your dog only growls, and *never* bites, you may be able to nip the behavior in the bud before you get nipped yourself by scolding or physically correcting the dog. If your dog is likely to bite, but you still want to try, talk to your veterinarian about temporary drug therapy to calm him sufficiently during initial training, and consider having your dog wear a muzzle.

You must cease and desist any of your behaviors that tell the dog he is the boss. As much pleasure as you may get from petting your dog absent mindedly as you watch TV, you can't. There will be no more free lunches, and no more free pets, for your dog. From now on, your dog must work for his petting, his praise, and even his food. The work will be simple—just obeying simple commands from you. He must sit when you tell him to sit, and wait until you have gone through doorways first. When he thrusts his head into your lap to be petted, you must ignore him. When you want to pet him, you must first have him obey some simple commands, and then pet him sparingly as a reward. Yes, it's tough love, but it may be an aggressive dog's only chance.

*Jacks and children raised to respect one another can become the closest of friends.*

### Jacks and Babies

Many a devoted dog owner has been known to get rid of the dog when a new baby comes home, often because of the stories they've heard about what dogs can do to babies. Just as many glibly bring the new baby home and hand it over to the dog to guard. Neither is the correct response. Dogs can hurt babies. They can also save babies. The way you introduce them may make the difference. Start now if you are expecting to add a baby to the home.

**1.** Your Jack should know how to come, sit, stay, and lie down on command.

**2.** Keep the dog on leash when first introducing him to the baby. If you are uneasy, you can muzzle the dog, but you don't want the dog to associate muzzling with the baby. This means it should already be familiar with the muzzle before the baby comes home and should sometimes wear it when not around the baby.

**3.** When first bringing the baby home from the hospital, keep the dog away. Let him get used to the sound and odor of the new family member. Some dogs may not understand this is a small human, not a prey animal, so be very careful at this time.

**4.** Have the dog sit and stay, bring the baby in the room, and reward the dog for staying. Gradually move the baby closer, all the while rewarding the dog for his good behavior.

**5.** Only when you feel confident about the dog should you allow him to sniff the baby.

**6.** Do not leave the dog and baby alone together.

**7.** Always make a fuss over the dog when the baby is present. Never shuttle the dog out of the room because the baby is coming in. You want the dog to associate the baby with good things coming, not to be jealous or resentful. Remember, your dog probably used to be the baby of the family.

Some dogs are afraid of children, either because they don't understand what they are or because they have had bad experiences with them. Introduce dogs and children carefully, encouraging the child to be gentle and to offer the dog a treat. Do not allow young children to sit on a dog, fall on him, or pull his hair, ears, or tail. Instruct children that they are never to run from the dog, scream shrilly around him, stare at him, or hurt him. It's not fair even to the most saintly of dogs to allow him to be picked on. Never take chances with a child's safety, but do give your dog a chance—safely.

# Obsessive Compulsive Disorder

Obsessive compulsive disorders (OCD's) are behaviors in which an animal is preoccupied with an irresistible urge to engage in an irrational act. Only recently has the extent of OCD been recognized in dogs. Because dogs of some breeds, including Jack Russell Terriers, seem more prone to develop OCD, a hereditary component may play a role. Most cases manifest themselves between three and twelve months of age. Examples of OCD behavior in dogs include incessant tail chasing, spinning, shadow chasing, digging, staring at spots, reflection staring, or self-mutilation. In some cases the owner inadvertently triggers the disorder by encouraging what at first seems to be a fun game or cute behavior— and in fact it is, except in those dogs that are predisposed to develop OCD. For example, many people find their dogs enjoy chasing a laser light dot shone on the ground. For most dogs, this is a fairly enjoyable game but they lose interest as soon as the light is turned off. For some dogs, and especially some Jacks, they become obsessed with looking for the light dot even after the game is over. They may spend hours running around the yard, ignoring all attempts of the owner to distract them with other games or even food, until they are exhausted. In some dogs, the obsessions become so overwhelming that they are no longer companions and may even endanger their own health.

Behavior modification alone is seldom successful. In the worst cases, euthanasia has been the only answer. Recent studies have shown that administration of the drug clomipramine hydrochloride (which acts to prolong the effect of serotonin, a chemical in the nervous system) significantly reduces compulsive behavior in dogs with OCD, although several weeks may be needed before improvements are seen. In addition, removing any stimuli that tend to elicit the compulsive behavior is also an important aspect of therapy.

*As with people, dogs can develop an astounding array of behavioral problems. No dog, and no owner, is perfect. Our dogs seldom act and do exactly as we would wish them to; we probably let them down even more. We try to change what we can, gripe about the rest, and love them regardless because the good more than makes up for the bad.*

## Chapter Seven

# A Good Mind to Do Something

Jack Russell Terriers have been popularized in large part because of their media exposure. Jacks do so well as screen stars not only because they are cute and clever, but also because they are mischievous. It's hard to teach a dog that never does anything to do a variety of tricks, but it's easy to teach a dog that does lots of things just when to do those things. This means that, from a Hollywood dog trainer's point of view, it's preferable to start with a dog that is constantly into everything and always trying out new behaviors. Then it is a comparatively easy matter to shape the dog so that he does those behaviors on command. Some of the most successful Jack actors had actually been given up by their initial owners, who found them too much to handle and too difficult to train. For the average pet owner, who may not be so motivated to shape unusual behaviors, these same dogs may be seen simply as incorrigible troublemakers!

Some of the beginning obedience exercises are difficult for Jack Russells,

*A canine mind is a terrible thing to waste.*

because they emphasize doing nothing. Exercises such as sitting, lying down, and staying can be tedious for a dog whose mind is racing with ideas. Your job is to make these exercises more exciting and rewarding, incorporating them into play and using lots of toys and treats for rewards.

## The Training Game

When Jack Russells are thinking their hardest, their tails are wagging just as hard. Dogs learn better both when they are thinking hard and having fun. This attitude won't come about because he's forced and punished into compliance. It comes about because his trainer knows how to make training into a game. Sometimes the game may be challenging, but it is always winnable.

Jacks Russells were bred to be stubborn. That ability to stick to task in the face of adversity is an essential trait in a dog that often finds itself in sticky situations that would have most other dogs turning tail or giving up. For Jack Russells, the tougher the challenge, the more they dig in their heels and resist. This means that the more you try to force them to do something, the greater their resistance.

In the old days when force-training methods were the accepted way, such dogs were labeled as stubborn and stupid. The Hollywood trainers knew better, and they could train these dogs to do just about anything because they didn't use force-training methods. They knew that to get a terrier to do what you wanted, it had to also be what he wanted. One way to do that is with the use of food and play as rewards.

## Food as Reward

Professional animal trainers and animal behavior scientists have shown that food training is highly effective. Food is used initially to guide the dog and later as a reward.

*The first step in training is to get your dog's attention.*

## ☆ JACK FACT ☆

**Clicker Training**
Professional dog trainers use a signal (such as a click sound) to instantly tell the dog when it has performed correctly. The signal is then followed by a food reward. A clicker signal is used because it is fast, noticeable, and something the dog otherwise does not encounter in everyday life. In order to apply this technique to the following instructions, whenever giving a reward is mentioned, you should precede it with a clicker signal. Even if you don't use a clicker, always precede any tangible reward with *"Good!"*

The dog is then gradually weaned from getting a food reward for each correct response, but instead is rewarded only at random correct responses. This random payoff is the same psychology used (very effectively) to induce people to put money (the correct response) into slot machines.

## Timing

Great dog trainers have great timing. The crux of training is anticipation: A dog comes to anticipate that after hearing a command, he will be rewarded if he performs some action, and he will eventually perform this action without further assistance from you. Your timing is everything; remember this sequence:

**1.** *Name.* Alert your dog that your next words are directed toward him by preceding commands with his name. Note that some dogs have a tendency to jump up in anticipation when using this technique.

**2.** *Command.* Always said with the same word in the same tone.

**3.** *Action.* Don't simultaneously place the dog into position as you say the command, which negates the predictive value of the command.

**4.** *Reward.* As soon as possible after the dog has performed correctly should come a signal *("Good!")* followed by a reward.

The sooner a reward follows an action, the better the association. It's sometimes difficult to reward a dog instantly, though, so you can do the next best thing by immediately signaling the dog a reward is coming. The best way to do this is with a noticeable sound the dog otherwise doesn't hear in everyday life, such as that from a clicker. The next best thing is to simply say *"Good!"* In either case, you give the signal just after the action and before the reward.

# Basic Training

It's never too early or too late to start the education of your terrier. With a very young pup, train for even shorter time periods than you would an adult. By the time your Jack reaches six months of age, he should know how to sit, down, stay, come, and heel. These exercises will be demonstrated with the help of a budding genius named Junior.

First, you have to get Junior's attention. Say *"Junior, watch me,"* and when he looks in your direction, say *"Good!"* and give him a treat or other reward. Gradually require Junior to look at you for longer and longer periods before rewarding him.

## Come

If Junior learns only one command, that command should be to come when called: it could save his life. He probably already knows how to come; after all, he comes when he's called for dinner. You want him to respond to *"Junior, come"* with that same enthusiasm; in other words, *"come"* should always be associated with good things.

Have a helper gently restrain Junior while you back away and entice him until he is struggling to get to you. Then excitedly call *"Junior, come!"* and turn and run away. Your helper should immediately release

*The sit-stay takes self-control!*

---

### ☆ **JACK FACT** ☆

**Slip or Choke Collars**

A choke collar is not for choking! In fact, it is more correctly termed a slip collar. The proper way to administer a correction with a choke collar is with a *very* gentle snap, then immediate release. The choke collar is placed on the dog so that the ring with the lead attached comes up around the left side of the dog's neck, and through the other ring. If put on backwards, it will not release itself after being tightened (you will be on the right side of your dog for most training). Never leave a choke collar on a dog! See page 89 for more information about collar choices.

---

him. When he catches you give him a special reward. Always keep up a jolly attitude and make him feel lucky to be part of such a wonderful game.

Next place Junior on lead, call *"Junior, come!"* and quickly run away. If he ignores you for more than a second, tug on the lead to get his attention, but don't drag him to you. After the tug, be sure to run backwards and make him think it was all part of the game.

Then place him on a longer line, allow him to meander about, and in the midst of his investigations, call, run backwards, and reward. After a few repetitions, drop the long line, let him mosey around a bit, then call. If he begins to come, run away and let him chase you as part of the game. If he doesn't come, pick up the line and give a tug, then run away as usual.

As Junior becomes more reliable, you should begin to practice (still on the long line) in the presence of distractions. Hold onto his leash just in case the distractions prove too enticing.

Some dogs develop a habit of dancing around just out of your reach, considering your futile grabs to be another part of this wonderful game. You can prevent this by requiring Junior to allow you to hold him by the collar before you reward him. Eventually you may add sitting in front of you as part of the game.

## Sit

*Sit* is the prototypical dog command, and with good reason. It's a simple way to control your dog and it's easy. The simplest way to teach the sit is to stand in front of your pup and hold a tidbit just above his eye level. Say *"Junior, sit,"* and then move the tidbit toward him until it's slightly behind and above his eyes. You may have to keep a hand on his rump to prevent him from jumping up. When he begins to look up and bend his hind legs, say *"Good!"* then offer the tidbit. Repeat this, requiring him to bend his legs more and more until he must be sitting before receiving the *"Good!"* and reward. If he backs up instead of sits down, place his rear against a wall while training.

## Stay

A dangerous habit of many dogs is to bolt through open doors. Teach your dog to sit and stay until given the release signal before walking

through the front door or exiting your car.

Have Junior sit, then say *"Stay"* in a soothing voice (if you precede a command with the dog's name they have a tendency to jump up in anticipation). If he tries to get up or lie down, gently but instantly place him back into position. Work up to a few seconds, give a release word *("OK!"),* praise and reward. Next, step out (starting with your right foot) and turn to stand directly in front of your dog while he stays. It's tempting to stare into your dog's eyes as if hypnotizing him to stay, but this really will have the opposite effect! Staring is perceived by the dog as a threat and can be intimidating, causing the dog to squirm out of position and come to you, his leader! Work up to longer times, but don't ask a young puppy to stay longer than 30 seconds. The object is not to push your dog to

---

### ☆ JACK FACT ☆

**Recall Rule**
Never have your Jack come to you and then scold him for something he's done. In his mind he is being scolded for coming, not for any earlier misdeed. Nor should you call your dog to you at the end of an off-lead walk. You don't want him to associate coming to you with relinquishing his freedom. Call him to you several times during the walk, reward and praise him, and then send him back out to play.

the limit, but to let him succeed. Finally, practice with the dog on lead by the front door or in the car. For a reward, take your dog for a walk!

## Down

When you need your Jack to stay in one place for a long time you can't expect him to sit or stand. This is when the *down* command really comes in handy.

Begin teaching the *down* command with the dog in the sitting position. Say *"Junior, down,"* then show him a tidbit and move it below his nose toward the ground. If he reaches down to get it, give it to him. Repeat, requiring him to reach farther down (without lifting his rear from the ground) until he has to lower his elbows to the ground. Never try to cram him into the down position, which can scare a submissive dog and cause a dominant dog to resist. Practice the *down/stay* just as you did the *sit/stay.*

## Heel

A pup's first experience walking on leash should be positive. Never drag a reluctant pup or let him hit the

*It's easiest to train your dog on a raised surface.*

end of the lead. Start by coaxing him a few steps at a time with food. When he follows you, praise and reward. In this way he begins to realize that following you while walking on lead pays off.

Once your pup is prancing alongside it's time to ask a little more of him. Even if you have no intention of teaching a perfect competition *heel,* your dog should know how to walk politely at your side.

Have Junior sit in heel position; that is, on your left side with his neck next to and parallel with your leg. If you line up your feet and your dog's front feet, that's close enough. Say *"Junior, heel"* and step off with your left foot first. During your first few practice sessions keep him on a short lead, holding him in heel position, and of course praising him. The traditional method of letting him lunge to the end of the lead and then snapping him back is unfair if you haven't first shown him what you expect. Instead, after a few sessions of showing his heel position, give him a little more loose lead and use a tidbit to guide him into correct position.

If your Jack still forges ahead after you have shown him what is expected, pull him back to position with a quick gentle tug, then release, of the lead. If, after a few days practice, he still seems oblivious to your efforts, then turn unexpectedly several times; teach him that it's his responsibility to keep an eye on you.

Keep up a pace that requires your dog to walk fairly briskly; too slow a pace gives him time to sniff and sight-see; a brisk pace will focus his attention upon you. Add some about-faces, right and left turns, and walk at different speeds. Teach him to sit every time you stop. Vary your routine to combat boredom. Be sure to give the *OK* command before allowing him to sniff, pull, and meander on lead.

# Higher Education

If you think obedience titles may be in your future, you might as well think big. Advanced obedience titles are well within reach of Jack Russell Terriers, who often relish the chance to do more active exercises than those involved in basic obedience. Many trainers find the best time to teach the advanced exercises is in the beginning. So rather than wait until your dog has earned the Novice degree, you may wish to introduce retrieving and jumping now.

Introduce your dog to the obedience dumb bells and gloves. Several advanced exercises require high and broad jumping. You can teach

*Every Jack should know at least one dog trick!*

that are tied down. Your dog will learn that the articles without your scent can't be picked up. Be careful you don't contaminate the other objects with your scent by touching them.

proper jumping style by giving your dog plenty of opportunity to jump low (and only low) jumps when he's younger. Only when he matures can you introduce slightly higher jumps. When he begins to seriously practice advanced exercise, vary the jump height so that your dog learns to judge height before jumping.

Even more advanced exercises will involve hand signals and scent discrimination. Again, there is no reason to postpone introducing these concepts to your dog. Teach hand signals just as you would voice signals; if your dog already knows voice signals, add hand signals by immediately preceding your standard voice command with a signal

For scent discrimination, get your dog used to using his nose to find hidden objects with your scent on them. Throw a scented object in the midst of several unscented objects

---

### ☆ JACK FACT ☆

**Jack Russell Training Rules**

• *Guide, don't force.* Forcing a Jack can cause him to resist, actually slowing down learning.

• *Once is enough.* Repeating a command over and over, or shouting it louder and louder, never helps a dog understand what is expected of him.

• *Give your dog a hunger for learning.* Your Jack will work better if his stomach is not full, and will be more responsive to food rewards. Never try to train a sleepy, tired, or hot dog.

• *Be a quitter.* Both you and your dog have good days and bad days. On bad days, quit. Never train your dog when you are irritable or impatient. Even on good days, don't push it. After about 15 minutes your dog's performance will begin to suffer unless a lot of play is involved. Keep your terrier wanting more.

• *The best laid plans don't include dogs.* Nothing ever goes as perfectly as it does in training instructions. Although there may be setbacks, you can train your Jack, as long as you remember to be consistent, firm, gentle, realistic, patient—and have a very good sense of humor.

Most Jacks find the basic obedience exercises boring, so teaching advanced exercises along with basic ones can help keep your dog's enthusiasm high. Another way to keep up enthusiasm is with fun dog tricks. Tricks are easy to teach with the help of the same obedience concepts outlined in the training section. Try these standards:

• Teach *roll over* by telling your dog to lie down, and then saying *"Roll over"* and luring him over on his side with a treat. Once he is reliably rolling on his side, use the treat to guide him on his back. Then guide him the rest of the way, eventually giving the treat only when he has rolled all the way over.

• Teach *catch* by tossing a tidbit or ball in a high arc over your dog's face. If he misses, snatch the tidbit off the ground before he can reach it. Eventually he'll realize that to beat you to the bounty he'll have to grab it before it reaches the ground.

• Teach *shake hands* by having your dog sit. Say *"Shake"* and hold a treat in your closed hand in front of your dog. Many dogs will pick up a foot to paw at your hand. These are the naturals! With others you have to give a little nudge on the leg, or lure his head far to one side so he has to lift the leg up on the opposite side. As soon as the paw leaves the ground, reward! Then require the dog to lift it higher and longer.

• Teach *speak* by saying *"Speak"* when it appears your Jack is about to bark. Then reward. Don't reward barking unless you've first said *"Speak."*

*Training is important for both good manners and safety in public.*

*Jacks and dog tricks are a perfect combination.*

# The Good Citizen

Half the fun of owning a Jack Russell Terrier is showing him off in public and including him in outdoor adventures. Half the problem of owning such a dog is that you attract attention wherever you go. People will stop to ask about your dog and will not be able to resist petting him. While this can be a great deal of fun and a wonderful way to meet people, it won't be much fun if your dog is barking or jumping all over everyone she meets, and it will be a bad reflection on the Jack Russell Terrier breed.

In order to formally recognize dogs that behave in public, the AKC offers the Canine Good Citizen (CGC) certificate, which requires your Jack to:

• accept a friendly stranger who greets you;
• sit politely for petting by a stranger;
• allow a stranger to pet and groom it;
• walk politely on a loose lead;
• walk through a crowd on a lead;
• sit and lie down on command and stay in place while on a 20-foot line;
• react politely to another dog and react calmly to distractions;
• remain calm when tied for three minutes in the owner's absence, under supervision by a stranger;

Remember that the most magnificent champion in the show or obedience ring is no credit to its breed if it is not a good public citizen in the real world.

# Class Acts

Good obedience classes are great aids for training your dog to behave properly at home, in public, and in competition. To find a good class, get referrals from other terrier trainers and sit in on the class. If the class uses outdated yank and jerk methods, look elsewhere. Your friend's well-being is worth too much.

If you plan on going on to compete in obedience, a class is a necessity. Obedience trials are held amidst great distractions. It would be nearly impossible for your dog to pass without having some experience working around other dogs. Obedience classes are filled with people who share many of your same interests. If you take the plunge into competition, class is a place to celebrate wins and laugh about failures.

Sometimes your Jack will be the star pupil. More often you will feel like the class delinquent. If you have a particularly unruly dog you may gauge your progress by simply being able to have your dog stand calmly beside you at the end of the course. Each dog will progress at its own pace; every dog will improve, and many dogs will profit from repeating the same class after using the first time through as a warm up.

Obedience classes train you to train your dog. Don't let your dog down. Remember, there is no such thing as an untrainable dog, only untrained dogs—-and whose fault is that?

## Chapter Eight

# Jack of All Trades

The best rewards of Jack Russell Terrier ownership are the intangible ones: sharing a wild adventure on forest hike, a special treat from the drive-thru window, a game of tag in the backyard, or a lazy evening snuggled in front of the television. You can share a perfect life with your Jack without ever entering any kind of competition, earning any kind of title, or winning any kind of ribbon. Many people, however, find that they enjoy activities with their Jack so much that they look for more challenges to share. Their pride in their partner is reflected by her accomplishments and memorialized by her titles. Their Jacks don't care about ribbons and records—they just think competitions are fun!

Jack Russells have lots of exciting competitions in which to dabble. From the comparatively sedate conformation shows and obedience trials to the rowdy earthdog trials and terrier races, there's something for everyone—and every Jack—to enjoy.

*Jack Russell Terriers are always in search of a new game.*

## A Day at the Rat Races

Racing is the most popular and spectacular of Jack Russell competitions. Six dogs break from a starting box, chase a lure (usually a scented fox tail) down the track and through a hole in some straw bales, where the lure stops and the dogs jump on it, often managing to get a grip on it despite the muzzles they wear. JRTCA sanctioned trials may be either flat races or steeplechases, both run in a straight line over a distance of 150 to 225 feet (46–69 m), with 200 feet (61 m) being average. The whole race lasts only a few seconds, but they're some of the most exciting seconds in any dog sport!

Even Jacks that have never seen a lure often go berserk at the sight of one speeding down the raceway. So if you are attending your first trial, a word of warning: Hold on tight! Jacks are notorious for their wild antics as spectators. They jump straight up in the air on spring loaded legs, barking their protests at being held back from the escaping varmint.

*Racing over hurdles is a favorite of Jacks and spectators alike.*

## Race Preparations

The fastest Jack will never live up to her potential without the best of nutrition, conditioning, and training. Race dogs are never fat! They need ample protein with which to build muscles, and ample exercise to turn that protein into muscles. Exercise should consist of both long walks and short sprints.

Although many adult Jacks that have never seen a lure have also proven themselves to be high caliber racers, the best time to train your Jack to race is when she is still a youngster. Don't practice in the heat of the day, or when your dog has just eaten or exercised. You don't want your dog to associate racing with being hot, uncomfortable, or tired.

**The pole-lure:** If you don't believe your Jack would deign to chase a lure, try this little experiment at home. Take a pole about six feet (1.8 m) long (a long horse lunging whip is best), and attach a string of about the same length to it. On the end of the string attach either a scrap of fake or real fur. Now run around your backyard, whipping the lure around erratically. Let your dog watch from the other side of a fence, or have someone hold her at first. Then, after your Jack has been whipped to a frenzy, let her loose and watch the fun begin. Don't let your dog jump too crazily, though. You don't want her to hurt herself in her enthusiasm. Let her catch the lure occasionally, but don't let it be too easy, and always quit with your dog wanting more. The pole-lure is an excellent training device for racing, but also

> ### ☆ JACK FACT ☆
>
> **Steeplechase**
> Steeplechases include four to six low hurdles (not over 8 inches [20 cm] for pups, or 16 inches [40 cm] for adults). Racers are divided according to age and height (over and under 12½ inches [31.8 cm], but still within the JRTCA standard of 10 to 15 inches [25–37 cm]).

makes a wonderful game and exercise device for everyday use.

In a race your Jack will be running in a straight line, so try to have a friend help you by holding the dog and releasing her only when you have a good head start. Don't try to drag the lure behind a car or even a bicycle; it's too dangerous, especially once your Jack actually catches up with the lure. The lure at a race is pulled on a long string that wraps around a large motor-driven wheel; lure machines are commercially available but few people invest in them. You can make a battery or hand-powered wheel if you are mechanically inclined.

**The muzzle:** Next, teach your JRT to play the game while wearing a muzzle. The muzzle must allow the dog to open her mouth so she can pant. Put the muzzle on her, let her run to catch the lure, and immediately remove the muzzle and let her catch the lure again unmuzzled. She will

quickly learn that the muzzle means fun, and that she'll also get a chance to bite the lure varmint at the end.

**The starting box:** The greater challenge is training the dog to break from the starting box. Start at home by walking your pup through a cardboard box. String the lure through it and practice letting your pup chase the lure through the box. Now loosely close the flap on the far end of the box and pull the lure through it. Raise the flap as the pup approaches. Gradually make your pup wait longer

*First one through the hole is the winner!*

for the flap to be opened, and reward her with a frolic after the lure. Don't let your pup cheat by going around the box! Eventually you will need access to a real box and lure, but this at-home training will give your dog a good head start. The official starting box is no more than 15 inches (37 cm) high, and has a front panel that is covered with wire or clear plastic so the dog can see out.

**The finish:** Also practice running the lure through a JRT-size hole between some straw bales (not hay bales, which are more solid). At races, the winner is determined according to which dog runs through the straw bale bottleneck first. Your dog must learn to dive right into it without hesitating. Start with a large hole and gradually decrease it to the size your dog will encounter at the races.

**The jumps:** If you want to enter steeplechases, introduce your Jack to jumping before the race. Jumping at full speed takes practice and experience. Start by running your lure over a series of low jumps; gradually work up until your dog is familiar with jumping the height she will encounter during the steeplechase.

**The competition:** The final step is running with other terriers, and if you have done your homework, your Jack is very likely to ignore her competitors and chase the lure with single-minded intent. In fairness to the other competitors, don't run your dog if you have any doubts about her ability to "run clean." If possible, try to run a practice race with one or two proven racers. Your dog may experiment by bumping or biting at them, but if they ignore her, she is more likely to join them in the chase.

**Running safety:** Some owners are reluctant to try racing because they fear their dog could be injured. True, any time your dog is active a certain risk is involved. But the risks in racing are minimal as long as your dog is in proper condition. Do not race your Jack if she doesn't get regular conditioning in the form of running during the week. If your dog has a previous injury, check with your veterinarian to make sure you don't risk re-injuring it. Remember, there is no such thing as halfway for a Jack Russell Terrier. Once she's out of the starting box, she will not run at half-speed or run half the distance. Make sure your dog is physically fit and sound or do not run your dog at all. Always limber your dog up before running, and walk her afterwards. On a hot day, you can soak your dog's coat with cool water before and after a race. If you expect to compete with your dog in an athletic event, be sure to treat her like the athlete she is.

# Show Off!

Conformation competition is similar to that at any dog show, with each dog evaluated in comparison to the standard of perfection. Type and soundness, with an emphasis on the structure necessary to do the job of a working JRT, are paramount. Conformation shows are still controver-

*Some pups are born show-offs.*

sial in some JRT circles. The Jack Russell Terrier is first and foremost a working terrier, not a beauty pageant contestant. The JRT standard was modeled after the best hunters of the day, with the idea that form follows function. Of course, real working ability involves so many intangibles that can never be evaluated in a show ring, or any place but the field. With these limitations in mind, no one can deny that a Jack that fits the standard is a striking animal that fills our eyes and our lives with beauty and pleasure. As long as conformation is never touted above ability, conformation dog shows can provide

an outlet in which Jacks can be compared to the standard and shown off to other Jack Russell Terrier enthusiasts who share an esthetic appreciation of these dogs.

## Show Training

The best of dogs won't be recognized in the few minutes the judge

> **TERRIER-IFIC!**
> An especially talented JRT is Camelot Derby, who holds the Bronze Medallion for Special Merit in the Field and twice won the JRTCA National Trial.

has to evaluate them unless that dog presents herself to her best advantage. Dogs should be trained to trot smartly beside you on lead, and to stand at attention. Discreet use of a squeaky toy, piece of fur, or liver is helpful in focusing the dog's attention and keeping her alert in the ring. Keep your Jack happy so that she doesn't let her tail drop while showing. Note that unlike many terrier breeds, JRT's are never sparred (faced off to each other to show gameness). Training for shows involves striking a balance between obedience and exuberance.

### Posing

Picture your Jack in the field at the moment she spies a squirrel in the distance. She is standing at attention, looking straight ahead, on her toes, with head and tail up and ears forward. You want to do your best to recreate this look in the ring, while at the same time having her stand with her legs in the show pose. The show pose is simply standing with the front legs parallel to each other and perpendicular to the ground, and the back legs also parallel to each other but set wider than the front legs, and with the hocks perpendicular to the ground. The head is held up and the tail is held up at an angle. The dog must be able to hold this pose even when the judge goes over her, looking at her bite and feeling her body, ears, legs, and tail.

In the ring the judge will often have the dog pose on an examination table for the individual exam. Accustom your dog to being on a table so she will be confident when placed on one at a show. Most dogs are hand-posed on the table, that is, the handler places their feet into position.

Your Jack should also know how to self-pose, which is customary when showing terriers on the ground. Begin by training your dog just as you would train her to do any other trick or exercise. Use a treat and have her stand in front of you, then say *"Pose,"* and give her the treat when she looks at it. Eventually you will require her to look at the treat for a few seconds before getting it, and then you will require her to step forward a step or two until she is closer to a show pose. Usually that means first working on stepping forward with the front legs so that she is stretched out a bit, rather than having her hind feet gathered under her. You can also use the treat to encour-

---

### *T E R R I E R - I F I C !*

A JRT with achievements that will never be equaled is Blencathra Badger, who won Best of Breed at the JRTCA National in 1985, the JRTBA National in 1987, the first Kennel Club Championship show in England in 1990, and the Crufts Centenary Show in 1991. He also earned three Field Hunting Certificates and sired many winning and working offspring. His most well-known offspring, however, is the TV star "Wishbone."

age her to stand with her feet parallel. Some dogs work better using a squeaky toy instead of bait. It's not uncommon for a dog to lose interest in food or toys in the hubbub of a dog show, which is why socialization and training classes are important. You can also use another dog in the ring to keep your dog on her toes. Many dogs assume a perfect show pose when they meet a strange dog, and if you can keep your dog under control and not interfering with the other dogs then this is another way to help your dog self-pose. This is not to be confused with sparring dogs; your Jack should never appear aggressive in the ring.

### ☆ JACK FACT ☆

**Just the Facts**
Contact the AKC for complete rules for AKC events, or read them online at *http://www.akc.org/insideAKC/resources/rulereg.cfm*

**Gaiting:** Posing is only half the fun. Dogs are also evaluated on how they move at a trot. Again, picture your Jack as she returns to you filled with pride carrying a prize she has dug up out of the yard. You want her to trot around with her head and tail up at a good, moderate pace. When the judge is looking at her movement head on or from the rear, you

*Stand at attention!*

**Dress for Success**

Several different show leads are available. Most Jack Russell handlers prefer a small choke collar and thin show lead. Experiment with different collar positions, which can influence the dog's head position and movement. Your dog will need to be perfectly show-groomed (see page 51), and you, too, should look professional in sports jacket or skirt. Be sure to wear flat rubber-soled shoes for running.

want her to be trotting in a dead straight line. This comes with practice, combined with play. It also requires you to be able to walk in straight line, a surprisingly difficult feat when trying to keep one eye on your dog.

**Practice:** From the dog's point of view, conformation showing is boring compared to the other JRT activities. More dogs perform poorly at shows from lack of exuberance than from over exuberance, so don't worry if your dog seems too playful. Make your Jack look forward to show practice. Bring lots of liver treats and a fur squeaky toy in the ring with you to keep your dog on her toes. Just don't distract the other dogs with them.

It will take many outings before both you and your Jack will give a polished performance. You can practice at informal matches meanwhile, and if you're lucky, join a handling class. There are professional handlers who will show your dog for you at AKC shows and probably win more often than you would; however, there's nothing like the thrill of winning when you're the one on the other end of the lead!

## JRTCA Shows

JRTCA conformation shows offer two groups of classes: Regular (which includes puppy, Open Adult, and working classes) and Miscellaneous. Puppy classes are divided by age (four to six month, six to nine month, and nine to twelve month), sex, and coat type, with class winners ultimately competing (through a series of elimination) for Puppy Conformation Champion and Reserve.

The Open Adult division may include Bred by Exhibitor and American Bred classes, the winners of which may eventually compete for Best Open Terrier and Reserve. Jacks that hold the Natural Hunting Certificate may enter the prestigious Working Division competition, which may be divided by height and coat. The class winners eventually compete for the ultimate award of JRTCA Working Terrier Conformation Champion and Reserve.

Other JRTCA classes emphasize the breeding value of a dog or family. The Stud Dog & Get class is based upon the merits and consistency of a sire shown along with two or three of his offspring. The Brood Bitch & Produce is a similar class for dams and offspring. Family classes may also be offered.

The Miscellaneous division may include optional classes for Novice (adult JRT's that have never placed in any regular class nor won a Novice class before), Neutered Dog, Spayed Bitch, Veteran (dogs over six years of age), Regional classes, Bronze Medallion Class (for JRT's that hold the JRTCA Bronze Medallion for Special Merit in the Field), and Suitability classes (for groundhog, red fox, grey fox, or raccoon/badger).

## AKC Shows

AKC shows offer the following classes: Puppy (which may be divided into classes for six to nine months and nine to twelve months), twelve to eighteen months, Novice, American Bred, Bred by Exhibitor, and Open. The Best of Breed class is only for dogs that are already Champions. All the male (dog) classes are judged before all the female (bitch) classes. Each class winner within a sex competes in the Winners class for points toward the championship title. Each time a judge chooses a dog as the best dog of its sex that is not already a Champion (in other words, either Winners Dog or Winners Bitch) it wins up to five points, depending upon how many dogs it defeats. To become an AKC Champion (Ch) a dog must win 15 points including two majors (defeating enough dogs to win three to five points at a time).

**At the show:** Get to the show early so you can get a feel for what's going on and get your dog acclimated, but don't get her overheated or tired. Locate your ring and watch the judge's pattern. Typically the dogs in each class will enter in numerical order according to armbands (pick yours up from the ring steward about 15 minutes before JRT's are to be judged) and pose while the judge checks them in and looks them over. Then the entire class will trot around once or twice. After that the judge will examine the first dog in line. The judge will then have that dog trot either directly away and back to him or her, or in a triangle. Then the procedure will be repeated until the last dog has been examined. After that all the dogs are posed again, and the judge may move them or switch them around or make some tentative picks. If you're

---

### ☆ JACK FACT ☆

**Therapy Dogs**

Some Jack Russell Terriers visit hospitals, nursing homes, mental health facilities, prisons, and other situations where they can provide people with unconditional love, motivation to communicate, entertainment, or just somebody warm and cuddly to hug. Therapy dogs must be meticulously well mannered and well groomed, and above all, friendly and utterly trustworthy. If someone grabs, yells at, or hugs a therapy dog too tightly, the dog must remain gentle and unperturbed. The Certified Therapy Dog letters are among the proudest a dog can attain.

*Show dogs must be clean and well-groomed.*

fortunate enough to win a ribbon, take it in stride; if not, take it in even better stride and congratulate the winner. One day that will be you.

Don't just fly back to your car or home after showing. Now that the pressure is off you'll find many people are eager to meet you and find out about your dog. Even after everyone has drifted off, take your dog on a tour of the dog supply stands and buy her a treat for being such a good sport. After all, your dog would probably have rather spent her day digging a hole and running amuck. Stay around and watch different handlers' grooming techniques and how they show their dogs. Watch the Terrier group and cheer on the Jack Russell Best of Breed (BOB) winner. Stay for Best in Show and cheer for the Terrier Group winner (hopefully the Jack Russell!) Don't make winning or losing the deciding factor as to whether you have a fun day at the show or not.

Almost everyone who enters a dog show loses that day, because the only dog that remains undefeated at the end of the show is the Best in Show winner. This means that you need to be able to separate your ego and self-esteem from your dog. You can't let your dog's ability to win in the ring cloud your perception of her true worth in her primary role: that of friend and companion. Because your Jack is undoubtedly a real member of your family and the apple of your eye, it can hurt to have her placed last in her class. Just be sure that she doesn't catch on and always treat her like a Best in Show winner whether she gets a blue ribbon or no ribbon at all. As long as you do that you will always be a winner at the end of the show.

## Junior Handling

Both the AKC and the JRTCA offer classes for young people in which the person's ability to present the dog is judged, rather than the dog's merit. Competitions for young people are a good way to instill confidence, poise, and good sportsmanship, as well as to give youngsters a goal and personal involvement in the day's activity. Perhaps one of them will grow up to become tomorrow's expert.

In the AKC this is called Junior Showmanship, and is for people ten to eighteen years of age. Classes are divided into Novice and Open, with Open classes for competitors who have won at least three first place wins in Novice. The classes may further be divided by age into Junior (ten to fourteen years) and Senior (fourteen to eighteen years) divisions.

In JRTCA shows, these competitions are called Youth Handler classes. They are open to somewhat younger children, with the Child Handler class open to children from five through nine years of age, and Junior Handler classes open to young adults from ten through sixteen years of age. These classes may also include the child's knowledge of the Jack Russell Terrier as well as their ability to present the dog as placement criteria.

JRTCA Youth division competition does not stop with conformation handling, but encourages youth participation in all facets of JRT competition, including obedience, go-to-ground, agility, and racing. The dogs

*T E R R I E R - I F I C !*
The first JRT to win an AKC title was CQH Daisy Mae of Starlight, CD, who also held a U-CDX degree with the United Kennel Club.

are never judged, but the handlers are judged on their knowledge of the dog and the rules and purpose of the sport, their ability to handle the dog effectively and kindly, and their ability to follow directions and rules.

# Mind Games

Part of the pleasure of living with Jack Russells is their keen ability to learn—which is not to say that they always do what you say! But given the proper motivation, a JRT can perform spectacularly, as has been ably demonstrated by the Jack Russells of media fame. Your dog may not have the chance to make it in the movies, but you can still show off her genius in obedience trials. The exuberant Jack especially profits from having her intellectual energy directed into acceptable behaviors.

In an obedience trial each dog's performance of a set group of exercises is evaluated against a standard of perfection. Several organizations, including the AKC, the United Kennel Club (UKC), and the JRTCA sponsor obedience trials, with progressively more difficult levels. AKC is the most popular venue in the United States, so will be the one described here.

UKC exercises are similar, but slightly more difficult. JRTCA obedience is similar to AKC obedience, offering sub-novice, novice, open, utility, brace, and junior handler classes. Sub-novice is similar to novice exercises, except the dog is on a leash. The brace class consists of two dogs performing the sub-novice exercises in tandem. The junior handler class also uses the sub-novice exercises.

## AKC Classes and Titles

No matter how smart your Jack is, you have to start with more elementary classes and earn those titles before moving on to more challenging—and fun—classes.

*Novice* is the lowest level of AKC competition. To earn the Companion Dog (CD) title a dog must qualify at three trials. Each qualifying score is called a "leg" and requires passing each individual exercise and earning a total score of at least 170 points out of a possible 200 points.

The *Novice* exercises are:
• Heel on lead, sitting automatically each time you stop, negotiating right, left, and about turns without guidance from you, and changing to a faster and slower pace;
• Heel in a figure eight around two people, still on lead;
• Stand still off lead 6 feet (1.8 m) away from you and allow a judge to touch it;
• Do the same heeling exercises as before except off-lead;
• Come to you when called from 20 feet (6 m) away, and then return to heel position on command;
• Stay in a sitting position with a group of other dogs, while you are 20 feet (6 m) away, for one minute; and
• Stay in a down position with the same group while you are 20 feet (6 m) away, for three minutes.

*Open* is the intermediate level of AKC competition. To be awarded the Companion Dog Excellent (CDX) title a dog must earn three legs performing these Open exercises:

*Obedience stars of the future?*

*The true Companion Dog is one that is your friend through good times and bad; be sure your Jack can say the same about you, even when he fails a trial!*

• Heel off lead, including a figure eight;
• Come when called from 20 feet (6 m) away, but dropping to a down position when told to do so part way to you, then completing the recall when called again;
• Retrieve a thrown dumbbell when told to do so;
• Retrieve a thrown dumbbell, leaving and returning over a high jump;
• Jump over a broad jump when told to do so;
• Stay in a sitting position with a group of dogs, when you are out of sight, for three minutes;
• Stay in a down position with a group of dogs, when you are out of sight, for five minutes.

*Utility* is the highest level of AKC competition. To earn the Utility Dog (UD) title a dog must earn three legs performing these Utility exercises:

• Heel, stay, sit, down, and come in response to hand signals;
• Retrieve a leather article scented by the handler from among five other unscented articles;
• Retrieve a metal article scented by the handler from among five other unscented articles;
• Retrieve a glove designated by the handler from among three gloves placed in different locations;
• Stop and stand on command while heeling and allow the judge to physically examine it with the handler standing 10 feet (3 m) away;
• Trot away from the handler for about 40 feet (12 m) until told to stop, at which point it should turn and sit, until directed to jump one of two jumps (a solid or bar jump) and return to the handler;
• Repeat the previous exercise, but jumping the opposite jump as before.

The Utility Dog Excellent (UDX) is awarded to a dog (which must already have its UD) that earns 10 legs in both Open (CDX) and Utility classes at the same trials.

The supreme AKC obedience title is the Obedience Trial Champion (OTCH). Unlike other obedience titles that require only performance to a standard proficiency, points toward the OTCH require performance of such precision that it is scored ahead of other passing dogs. A dog that places first or second in either Open or Utility classes earns a certain number of points depending on how many dogs were in competition. It takes 100 points, plus three first placements, to earn the OTCH; understandably, very few dogs in any breed can claim such a prestigious title.

If you enter competition with your Jack Russell, keep in mind that in years to come the times you failed will bring you the best stories and the fondest memories. After all, passing is boring compared to the imaginative ways your Jack can think of to fail! So be grateful for your passing scores, but enjoy your failing ones—they're the ones that really capture your Jack's spirit.

# Jumping Jack Flashes

Agility competition combines obedience, athleticism, and excitement. Dogs jump, climb, weave, balance, and run through tunnels in a race against the clock. Jack Russell Terriers love the challenge and have the mental and physical attributes to place them among the top contenders at this new sport.

The AKC, JRTCA, United States Dog Agility Association (USDAA) and United Kennel Club (UKC) sponsor trials and award titles. We will describe the AKC program here, although all the programs are similar in concept.

## AKC Agility

The obstacles are arranged in various configurations that vary from trial to trial. Handlers can give unlimited commands but cannot touch the obstacles or dog, or use food, toys, whistles, or any training or guiding devices in the ring. Points are lost for refusing an obstacle, knocking down a jump, missing a contact zone, taking obstacles out of sequence, and exceeding the allotted time limit. To get a qualifying score a dog must earn 85 out of a possible 100 points with no nonqualifying deductions.

Classes are divided by height, with Jacks competing in either the 12-inch (30 cm) jump height class (for dogs 14 inches [35 cm] and under at the withers) or the 16-inch (40 cm) jump class (for dogs 18 inches [45 cm] and under at the withers). Some very short Jacks might compete in the 8-inch (20 cm) jump class, for dogs 10 inches (25 cm) and under at the withers.

The obstacles and their requirements are:

• The A-Frame requires the dog to climb over two 8 or 9 feet (2.4 or 2.7 m) long boards, each 3 to 4 feet (1–1.2 m) wide, positioned so they form an A-frame with the peak about 5 to 5½ feet (1.5–1.7 m) off the ground.

• The Dog Walk requires the dog to climb a sloping panel and walk across a suspended section and down another sloping panel. Each panel is 1 foot (30 cm) wide and

*Introduction to the tire jump.*

**Search and Rescue**

Search and Rescue (SAR) teams may search over miles of wilderness to find a lost child or through tons of rubble to discover a buried victim. SAR dogs must respond to commands reliably, negotiate precarious footing, follow a trail and locate articles, and most of all, use air scenting to pinpoint the location of a hidden person. National and local canine search and rescue teams are available for local emergencies, and may also be prepared to fly across country in the cases of disasters. Nimble Jack Russell Terriers are especially adept at seeking out buried victims.

either 8 or 12 feet (2.4 or 3.7 m) long, and the horizontal bridge section is 3 or 4 feet (90 or 120 cm) high.

• The Seesaw requires the dog to traverse the entire length of a 1 foot (30 cm) wide by 12 feet (3.7 m) long sloping panel supported near its center by a fulcrum base, so that when the dog passes the center the plank teeters to rest on its other end.

• The Pause Table requires the dog to stop and either sit or lie down for five seconds on top of a table approximately 3 feet (90 cm) square, with the height varying according to the height class (8 inches [20 cm] for Jacks 12 inches [30 cm] and under; 16 inches [40 cm] for taller Jacks).

• The Open Tunnel requires the dog to run through a flexible tube, about 2 feet (60 cm) in diameter and 10 to 20 feet (3–6 m) long, and curved so that the dog cannot see the exit from the entrance.

• The Closed Tunnel requires the dog to run through a lightweight fabric chute about 12 to 15 feet (3.7–4.6 m) long, with a rigid entrance of about 2 feet (30 cm) in diameter.

• The Weave Poles require the dog to weave from left to right through an entire series of 6 to 12 poles, each spaced 20 to 24 inches (50–60 cm) apart.

• The Single Bar Jumps require the dog to jump over a high jump consisting of a narrow bar without knocking it off. Note: Other single jumps are also permitted.

• The Panel Jump requires the dog to jump over a high jump consisting of a solid appearing wall without displacing the top panel.

• The Double Bar Jump (or Double Oxer) requires the dog to jump two parallel bars positioned at the jump heights specified for the Single Bar Jump, and situated a distance of one-half the jump height from each other.

• The Triple Bar Jump requires the dog to jump a series of three ascending bars, in which the horizontal distance between adjacent bars is one-half the jump height and the vertical distance is one-quarter the jump height.

• The Tire Jump (or Circle Jump) requires the dog to jump through a circular object (approximately 2 feet [60 cm] in diameter) resembling a tire suspended from a rectangular frame, with the bottom of the opening at the same height as the Single Bar Jump.

• The Window Jump requires the dog to jump through a 2-foot (60 cm) square (or diameter) window opening with the bottom of opening at the same height as the Single Bar Jump.

• The Broad Jump requires the dog to perform a single jump over a spaced series of either four 8-inch (20 cm) or five 6-inch (15 cm) wide sections.

Because safety is of utmost importance, all official jumps have easily displaceable bars in case the dog fails to clear them. All climbing obstacles have contact zones painted near the bottom that the dog must touch rather than jumping off the top. All contact equipment surfaces are roughened for good traction in both dry and wet weather.

**AKC classes:** AKC agility is divided into two types, the standard agility classes that include all the obstacles, and Jumpers With Weaves (JWW) agility classes. The latter is a faster paced version of agility that emphasizes jumping and speed without the careful control needed for the pause table and contact points in the standard obedience class. Titles for the standard agility classes are NA for Novice, OA for Open, and AX for Excellent, and MX for Master. JWW titles are the same with a "J" added to the end (NAJ, OAJ, AXJ, and MXJ).

For standard agility:

The *Novice* class uses 12 to 13 obstacles, including the A-Frame,

*Whew! Made it over the Dog Walk.*

Pause Table, Dog Walk, Open Tunnel, Seesaw, Closed Tunnel, Broad Jump, Panel Jump, Double Bar Jump, either the Tire Jump or Window Jump, and two or three additional obstacles (excluding the One Bar and Triple Bar Jumps).

The *Open* class uses 15 to 17 obstacles, including the ten mandatory obstacles from the Novice class plus Weave Poles and four to six additional obstacles. The latter may include one Triple Bar Jump but cannot include the One Bar Jump.

The *Excellent* class uses 18 to 20 obstacles, including all the Open Class obstacles (except that the Broad Jump is optional) plus the Triple Bar Jump, One Bar Jump, and additional jumps or tunnels to meet the required number of obstacles.

For Jumpers With Weaves classes:

The *Novice JWW* class uses 13 to 15 obstacles, including one Double Bar Jump, one series of six Weave Poles, and the remainder Single Bar Jumps.

The *Open JWW* class uses 16 to 18 obstacles, including one Double Bar Jump, one Triple Bar Jump, one series of six to 12 Weave Poles, and the remainder Single Bar Jumps and One Bar Jumps.

The *Excellent JWW* uses 18 to 20 obstacles, one Double Bar Jump, one Triple Bar Jump, one series of ten to 12 Weave Poles, and the remainder Single Bar Jumps and One Bar Jumps.

In addition, the courses may optionally include the Open Tunnel, Closed Tunnel, Broad Jump, Panel Jump, Tire Jump, and Window Jump.

It gets harder, though. One of the major challenges of an agility course is the complex course the dog must take from obstacle to obstacle. This course includes tougher challenges at higher levels of competition. For example, the obstacles may have to be approached from sharp angles (up to 90 degrees in Novice, 135 degrees in Open, and 180 degrees in Excellent). Courses may also include Call-Offs, in which the dog must not jump an obstacle in its path, Options and Traps, in which the dog must jump only one of two obstacles at a decision point, Side-Switches, in which the course makes an "S" curve, requiring the handler to switch from one side of the dog to the other, and Lead-Out Advantages, in which handlers who can run ahead of their dogs while the dog remains steady at the start line or pause table are at an advantage.

## JRTCA Agility

JRTCA, unlike other agility competitions, offers competition for dogs on lead. Leashes are used only to direct the dog and as insurance that she won't get excited and run off; the leash is not to force her to perform the obstacles. Novice On-lead classes are for dogs that have never earned a score of at least 190 points out of the possible perfect 200 points in any agility competition. Dogs that have earned such a score must be shown in Advanced On-lead competition. An On-lead Agility certificate is awarded to dogs that have received three scores of over 170 points in either Novice or Advanced classes. The JRTCA offers the titles of Agility I Certificate, Agility II Certificate, and Agility III Certificate to dogs that pass progressively more difficult off-lead courses. The Agility High Score Champion and Reserve are awarded to the Jacks with the best combined scored of Agility I and Agility II at a given competition

## Training

Many obedience clubs are now sponsoring agility training, but you can start some of the fundamentals at home. Entice your dog to walk through a tunnel made of sheets draped over chairs; guide her with treats to weave in and out of a series of poles made from several plumber's helpers placed in line; make her comfortable walking on a wide raised board; teach her to jump through a tire and over a hurdle. Teach her some basic obedience (sit, down, come, and stay) and make sure she's comfortable and under control around other dogs.

You need to condition your Jack like any athlete to compete in agility. You also need to have a health check beforehand, making sure your dog is not lame, arthritic, or visually impaired. High jumping and vigorous weaving can impose stresses on immature bones so these should be left until adulthood.

# Follow Your Nose

The way to start training your dog depends upon what motivates your dog. For chowhounds you can begin by walking a simple path and dropping little treats along it. The dog will soon learn that it can find treats simply by following your trail. As training progresses, the treats get dropped farther and farther apart.

Of course the actual tracking tests will require considerably more training than this, but once you have taught your dog to follow its nose, you're on the right track!

### AKC Tracking

The AKC offers several tracking titles:

The AKC Tracking Dog (TD) title is earned by following a 440 to 500 yard (402–457 m) track with three to five turns laid by a person from 30 minutes to two hours before.

The Tracking Dog Excellent (TDX) title is earned by following an "older" (three to five hours) and longer (800 to 1,000 yard [732–914 m]) track with five to seven turns, with some more challenging circumstances. One of these circumstances is the existence of cross tracks laid by another track layer about 1½ hours after the first track was laid. In addition, the actual track may cross various types of terrain and obstacles, including plowed land, woods, streams, bridges, and lightly traveled roads.

The Variable Surface Tracking (VST) title is earned by following a three to five hour track, 600 to 800 yards long, over a variety of surfaces such as might be normally encountered when tracking in the real world. At least three different surface areas are included, of which at least one must include vegetation and at least two must be devoid of vegetation (for example, sand or concrete). Tracks may even go through buildings, and may be crossed by animal, pedestrian, or vehicular traffic.

### JRTCA Tracking

The JRTCA offers Trailing and Locating trials, which are better suited for the Jack Russell Terrier. Trailing and Locating is a JRTCA competition that requires dogs to follow a scent through a short tunnel and an open area to locate a simulated quarry. Start with very short trails, gradually working backwards, further from the quarry. JRT's are natural sniffers, and most catch on quickly as long as it leads to fun.

## Chapter Nine

# The Jack Russell Underground

The leaves rustle in the trees on a crisp autumn day as you and your Jack enjoy a brisk hike in the woods. What may seem to be a good opportunity for a relaxing stroll to you is a great opportunity for a wild hunt for your JRT. Whether or not hunting is in your blood, it's in your Jack's blood, and you'd better be ready to deal with it, either by embracing hunting as your own new pastime or knowing what to do when your terrier goes hunting without you.

## The Terrier Hunting Companion

The JRT at your side is the product of generations of selective breeding to produce a dog having both the physical and mental abilities to seek out, chase, and follow quarry below ground, and to stay with it until the quarry bolts, is dug out, or the hunter calls the dog. If your Jack follows an animal to ground without your knowledge, she could remain there for days. It goes against her nature to

*Jacks love to dig in!*

give up and go home. This never-say-quit attitude is great for a hunting terrier, but can prove disastrous if you can't locate your dog. When walking or hunting in an area with denning wildlife, your terrier should always wear a remote locator collar (see page 120).

### On the Hunt

If you are interested in hunting with your JRT it's best to find an experienced hunting terrier person who can show you the ins and outs of local hunting areas and help ensure the safety of your dog. Find out about your local laws and hunting seasons; in many areas it is illegal to hunt mammals with dogs at any time. Hunting is serious business, and not something to be undertaken on a whim. Your dog must be in top shape with good muscle tone and the ability to keep up a good day's work. Every region of the country has its own particular dangers from animals, plants, land features, and man-made dangers such as poisons, traps, automobiles, and hunters. Know them before venturing out into the wilds. Ask your veterinarian about any special vaccination precautions. Your hunting

*Hunting Jacks follow their noses—sometimes into trouble. Be prepared.*

backpack should include a first aid kit, flash light, towels, dog food, water, a metal dowel, an assortment of digging tools, and extra batteries for your remote collar.

On the first hunt let your dog take his cues from a more experienced hunting terrier if possible. Most terriers find hunting is far more fun than fighting, so hunting terriers seldom fight in the field. You should also spend your first few hunts with your terrier on leash, until he understands all the ground rules—especially the ones about sticking around and coming when called.

Once a den is located don't force your Jack into the hole. Let the dog make the choice to proceed at his own pace. Most Jacks will leap right into the action and instinctively work the quarry. If the animal doesn't bolt, and your terrier stays true to his heritage and doesn't budge, you'll probably have to start digging. Use the metal dowel to form an air passage into the tunnel through which to listen and pinpoint your terrier's position from its baying. Be very careful and dig slowly as you near the animals. The exception is if your dog seems to have cornered a skunk, in which case time is of the essence.

## ☆ JACK FACT ☆

**Locator Collars**

Your Jack should always wear a remote locator collar anytime she may go underground. This collar emits a radio signal that is picked up by a handheld receiver, which the operator then uses to locate the position of the terrier. Before these collars were available the only way to find a dog underground was through careful listening—still a handy skill to have in the field.

Remaining in an enclosed space with skunk spray can cause a deadly reaction from inhaling the toxic fumes. If possible, upon reaching the dog and his quarry, block the quarry from the dog and lift the dog out of the hole. This depends on what kind of animal is cornered; with some you will want to grab your dog by the tail, pull him away, and get to safety as quickly as possible. In many cases the quarry can then proceed about its business unharmed, although if you again release your dog anywhere in the area he will likely take up where he left off and once again corner the same animal.

# Hunting Titles

The JRTCA has always promoted hunting skills as the prime attribute of the Jack Russell Terrier. Accordingly, that association's most prestigious titles are reserved for dogs that have proved their mettle in the field. The JRTCA awards the *Sporting Certificate* to terriers that perform successfully either in man-made structures or with nonformidable prey (such as squirrels or rats) in a period spanning at least one year. The owner and another JRTCA member must certify they have accompanied the dog hunting at least four times, and that the dog regularly hunts.

The *Natural Hunting Certificate Below Ground in the Field* is awarded to terriers that perform successfully in natural terrain with fox,

---

## ☆ JACK FACT ☆

**Lost Underground**

Your terrier should always be wearing a locator collar whenever he goes into an area where animal burrows are found. If your Jack is lost while he's not wearing a collar, and you suspect he could be stuck in a hole, look for burrows with evidence of digging or entry. If possible, use another Jack with hunting experience, who will often go to the same hole (just don't let this dog out of your sight). Walk very quietly and listen for rustling or barking. Calling your dog seldom helps, because most dogs will stop barking so they can listen— meaning you can walk right past your listening dog. Don't give up—some terriers have been found after a week or more underground. When you find a likely hole, dig very carefully. A collapsed hole can fill the entrance with dirt, suffocating the entombed dog below.

---

badger, woodchuck, raccoon, and in some cases, opossum. For obvious reasons, skunks are never acceptable! To do this, a Jack must enter a natural earth den and locate quarry on its own; having found it, he must mark it (by barking or otherwise alerting the hunter) and either bolt it (flush it from the den), draw it (pull it from the den), or stay with it until the hunter digs it out. This must be accomplished in front of a JRTCA working judge. If a JRT performs successfully with quarry of three different formidable species it is awarded the supreme working title: the JRTCA *Bronze Working Terrier Medallion for Special Merit in the Field*.

The American Working Terrier Association (AWTA) issues the *Working Certificate (WC)* with requirements similar to those for the JRTCA's Natural Hunting Certificate Below Ground in the Field. The AWTA also awards the *Hunting Certificate (HC),* which is issued to terriers regularly used for hunting game such as rabbits, squirrels, opossums, rats, raccoons, muskrats, or even for flushing and/or retrieving upland birds over a full hunting season.

**Note:** These titles require a terrier to work, but not necessarily kill, the quarry.

---

### ☆ JACK FACT ☆

**Skunked!**

If a skunk sprays your Jack, take her to open air immediately and wash as much of the spray off her body as possible. Commercially available products such as *Skunk Off!* are handy for carrying in the field. If the dog has been enclosed in a den with a skunk, she could become overcome by the toxic fumes, and could even lose consciousness or have convulsions within minutes. In severe cases you may have to administer mouth to mouth breathing.

---

# Get Down and Dirty

Every Jack Russell Terrier may yearn for a day in the field rooting out vermin, but not every Jack owner shares that enthusiasm. Terrier trials provide the perfect venue in which both dogs and owners can share a splendid afternoon. Your dog can hunt under safe conditions, without harming any animals, while you relax and share the camaraderie of good friends. Trials conducted by the AKC are known as Earthdog trials; those held by the JRTCA are Go-to-Ground trials. These trials enable terriers that would not otherwise have a chance to prove themselves in the field to demonstrate their instincts and abilities. These trials are designed to simulate the conditions a terrier might encounter in the field, requiring her to enter a tunnel and proceed down it and around corners until she finds a caged rat, which she should then "mark" by scratching, barking, whining, or digging for a sustained time period. Not only is the rat caged, but the cage is behind a barrier so that no harm can possibly come to the rat.

## Training

Don't be discouraged because your dog has never even seen a rat or gone underground. True, it's always easiest to start with a youngster, but you can do the same thing with a Jack of any age.

**Introduction to rats:** Trying to introduce a dog to a rat amid the confusion of a terrier trial can be frustrating. It's better to introduce your dog to the rat in a location that the dog is already comfortable in. Place the rat in a small, secure cage. Make a big deal out of showing the rat to her, excitedly whispering *"Rat!"* while keeping it just out of her reach. Most dogs will be cautious at first, which is only normal and smart. Don't rush her. Let her approach the cage on her own time. She may creep forward to examine the caged beast. Let her get a good look and sniff, and then gradually move the cage about, even going toward her if she is particularly brave, teasing the dog without frightening her. Don't be discouraged if your pup shows little interest; terriers develop their predatory instincts at different ages, and she may just need to grow up some more.

You can increase your dog's barking by holding her back from the cage once she has decided she really wants it. Hold her by her body, rather than her collar, as many dogs have learned a tug on the collar means to settle down. The more frustrated she is, the more she will bark, and barking is essential for an earthdog. Reward barking by letting her have a quick bite at the cage (making sure she cannot touch the rat), and then restrain her again.

Always take care that the rat cannot be injured in any way. Be especially careful of its toes or tail that may protrude from the cage, and be mashed or hurt. Most rats grow accustomed to the dogs barking, but they will never grow accustomed to

physical abuse or neglect. Drag a fur piece if you want a moving lure. Allowing your terrier to practice by killing a tame laboratory rat is considered neither sporting nor effective. Remember, JRT's were not bred to kill, and killing is not part of a terrier trial.

**Introduction to tunnels:** You don't need a rat to get started accustoming your pup to some of the conditions she will encounter at a trial (although it does help). You

---

### ☆ JACK FACT ☆

**Coonhound Paralysis**
Don't be misled by the name. Jack Russell Terriers can get it too. Coonhound paralysis is a neurological condition that some, but not all, dogs contract following a raccoon bite. Experimental evidence suggests that some dogs are susceptible to a component of raccoon saliva, whereas other dogs injected with the same saliva are not affected. Signs appear seven to eleven days after a raccoon bite, and include weakness, usually progressing to paralysis. Paralysis may last several weeks to several months. With good nursing care the prognosis is good, although some severely affected dogs can die of respiratory paralysis. Recovered dogs are as likely, or perhaps even more likely, to develop the condition again if again bitten by a raccoon.

can start a young pup even without a real tunnel. Just use a couple of cardboard boxes and drag a fur toy on a string through them, enticing your terrier to follow. Let her catch it and then have a good game of tug o' war while she's still in the box. Most Jacks will dive right in if a game is involved, but you may have to use food for more reticent dogs. The best enticement is the caged rat

you've already introduced to your terrier. Just don't resort to stuffing the dog in! Instead, get a bigger box and start over. When she's running through the makeshift box without hesitation, it's time to move to a better tunnel.

Depending on your pup's size, you may be able to buy a 5-foot (1.5 m) section of drain pipe and secure it on top of the ground. If you can't find one, you can use straw bales to fashion tunnels in your yard, or you can make your own tunnels (or liners, as they are called) using wood for the sides and top, keeping the natural earth floor. You'll want to do this eventually. Start with the liners above ground, and use only a short, straight section. Then gradually add more distance and a turn or two. If your liner has a removable top you can run a string through the tunnel with a toy on it and lead your terrier through it. The size of the tunnels in a trial are 9-inch by 9-inch (22.5 cm by 22.5 cm); you can start a little larger and then work down toward the narrower size. If you really don't mind destroying your yard (and let's face it, your Jack has probably already done that for you) you can sink your liners into the ground so the tops are flush with ground level. But a warning: This only works on high ground; otherwise the tunnels will be flooded with the first good rain. Note, too, that this may well be the final step in convincing your neighbors that you are more than a little odd.

**Rats!** If you have a caged rat, place it at the far end of the tunnel,

*A simple way to make a homemade tunnel is with hay bales.*

tell your dog *"Rat!"* and show him the rat through the tunnel opening. Use a barricade so he can't run around the tunnel to the rat. If he still won't go through, string a line through the tunnel and gently drag the caged rat through it; this is usually sufficient to get the most recalcitrant terrier right in the tunnel. It's tempting to give your terrier a nudge, or even a shove, to get it started, but being pushed into a closed space is alarming for any dog and will only result in greater reluctance to enter. When your terrier does get to the caged rat, reward him by letting him bark and bite at the cage for a moment.

Once your terrier is charging through the tunnel without hesitation, introduce a turn at the very beginning. At first the turn should be only a foot from the entrance of the tunnel, so he can practically see the daylight through the other end by poking his head way in and peering around.

Soon he will understand that lack of daylight just means another turn is up ahead.

The next training step is to introduce animal scent to the liner. Various animal scents are available at any hunting store. If you happen to have a pet rat you can make homemade eau d'rat from its used bedding. Put the bedding in a jar, add water, let it ferment for a few days, and then put the solution in a sprayer. Spray the scent in a path leading to the caged rat. At this point the rat cage should be behind bars that prevent the dog from actually biting the cage.

## Digging Deeper

Only after your Jack is doing well in the aboveground tunnels should you begin to repeat the entire process with underground tunnels. The transition to working underground is more difficult than you might imagine, and some terriers will try to get to the rat without having to go underground. Never allow your dog to reach and work the cage rat from anywhere but the tunnel. Gradually back away from the entrance so you are releasing your Jack farther and farther from it. Increase the distance and turns in the tunnel. Practice removing your terrier from the

---

### ☆ JACK FACT ☆

**Working or Sporting Terrier?**
The historically correct use of the term "working terrier" refers to a terrier that has actually proven itself by facing its quarry underground, within the dark confines of a tunnel or den. The designation of "sporting terrier" is more appropriate for terriers that have only hunted aboveground.

---

tunnel quickly and gently from a removable panel just in front of the rat cage. Remove your dog by grasping her neck scruff with one hand and placing the other under her chest. Finally, don't practice too much! Jack Russells aren't dumb. At some point they will grow weary with the rat they can never have, and their enthusiasm will dampen. This may take ten years for some dogs, or ten sessions for others. Since you don't know when your dog may tire, take it easy at least until she's earned her earthdog titles.

## Training Opportunities

Many owners don't have the facilities to make a home practice course, and even those Jacks with this advantage may still need some further introduction. The AKC *Introduction to Quarry* class was designed for just this purpose. Dogs need no training to participate, and the purpose is to make it a positive experience for the dog. The handler releases the dog ten feet from the tunnel entrance and then stands quietly beside the entrance. The tunnel is 10 feet (3 m) long with one 90-degree turn. The natural instincts of most Jacks propel them right into the tunnel until they come face to face with the first rodent many of them have ever seen. Many Jacks will instinctively bark and work the quarry, but others remain hesitant. With some encouragement from the judge most catch on quickly and subsequently have to be pulled from the tunnel under protest, still slinging threats at the rat that so rudely ignored them. Those dogs that reach the quarry within two minutes and work it for 30 seconds receive a passing score. However, as this class does not lead to a title, passing or failing is not the important factor here; leaving the trial with a terrier itching to do it again is the real reward. Now let the games begin!

# AKC Earthdog Tests

The AKC offers three increasingly challenging levels of earthdog testing after the Introduction to Quarry, leading to the Junior, Senior, and Master Earthdog titles.

In the *Junior Earthdog* test, the terrier is released ten feet from the tunnel entrance but the handler must remain at the release point. The dog has 30 seconds to traverse the 30-foot-long (9.1 m) tunnel with its three 90 degree turns and reach the quarry, which it must then work continuously for one minute. The dog must qualify twice to earn the Junior Earthdog title. Jacks that are fast and frenzied workers have no problem earning the Junior title; however, subsequent titles that require more self-restraint can be trickier!

To earn the *Senior Earthdog* title the testing gets considerably tougher and more like what a dog would encounter in a real hunting situation. Now the dog is released 20 feet (6 m) from the entrance, which is steeper and somewhat hidden. The terrier is also faced with a false entrance: a tunnel that does not lead to the quarry. The dog must use the scent trail to choose the correct entrance. The design of this tunnel is the same as that for the Junior test, with two

*Even youngsters have the urge to explore the underworld.*

*I know you're in there!*

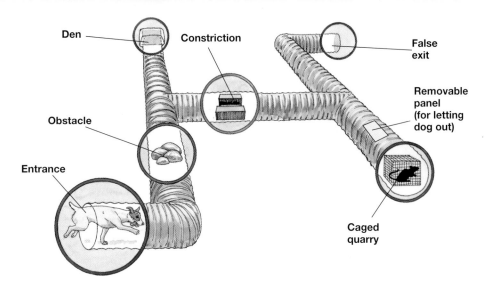

Den — Constriction — False exit

Removable panel (for letting dog out)

Obstacle

Entrance

Caged quarry

tricky differences: a false exit that goes for about 7 feet (2.1 m) and has one right angle turn, and a tunnel leading to a false den that contains bedding but no rat. The dog has 90 seconds to reach the real rat and must work it for another 90 seconds. After that the rat is blocked from the dog's view and removed; then the handler calls his dog back through the tunnel. This simulates the field situation in which the quarry bolts from the den. A dog that refuses to leave the den when called is a serious liability in the field. The dog must leave the tunnel within 90 seconds to pass. Dogs that pass the Senior level test three times are crowned Senior Earthdogs and can now compete in an even more challenging test.

The *Master Earthdog* test adds more elements that would be found in a real hunting situation. In an actual hunt a dog usually hunts together with another, often unfamiliar, dog, and must often search over

great distances for a den entrance. For the Master test, two terriers are released about 100 feet (30.5 m) from the tunnel entrance, which is somewhat hidden and blocked with a removable obstruction. An unscented false tunnel is located along the scent line leading to the real tunnel. The dogs have one minute to locate the correct entrance, whereupon one dog is staked out while the other is allowed to enter the tunnel. Just as in a real underground den, the tunnel contains a couple of surprises: a constriction point where the tunnel narrows to only 6 inches (15 cm) wide, and an obstruction posed by a 6-inch (15 cm) diameter pipe that can be moved by the dog 2½ inches (6.2 cm). The dog has 90 seconds to reach the quarry, and must work it for another 90 seconds, during which time tapping noises simulating the hunter digging to the quarry are made by the judge. Meanwhile the staked (or honoring) dog should remain reasonably quiet; the two dogs will switch places once the first one is finished. A terrier must qualify at four trials to add the prestigious Master Earthdog title to its name.

# JRTCA Go-to-Ground Trials

The JRTCA Go-to-Ground trials offer three class divisions: Novice, Open, and Certificate. The novice and open divisions are divided into puppy and adult classes, and the certificate division is divided by height into those dogs of standard height either under or over 12½ inches (31 cm).

The *Novice* division consists of a 10-foot (3 m) tunnel with one turn. To pass the dog must reach the rat within one minute and work it for another half minute. The dog may leave the tunnel and re-enter several times, as is often typical of an inexperienced dog seeking direction or confidence.

After passing at the Novice level, terriers can compete in the *Open* division, in which the tunnel is 30 feet (9.1 m) long with two turns. The dog must reach the quarry in only 30 seconds and work it for an additional minute. They can only leave and

*More advanced levels have less obvious tunnel entrances.*

re-enter the tunnel once. Dogs that pass in the Open division are eligible for the JRTCA *Trial Certificate.*

Puppies that have passed at the Open level can compete at the *Puppy Championship* level, with requirements the same as in the open division. The *Certificate* division is only for adult Jacks that have passed at the Open level. The requirements are the same as for the Open level except that the terrier may not leave the earth once she has entered.

# American Working Terrier Association (AWTA) Tests

The AWTA offers the Novice class for beginners, in which the tunnel is 10 feet long with one right angle turn. The dog is released 10 feet (3 m) away from the tunnel's entrance and has one minute to reach the quarry (two minutes for half credit), which she must then work for 30 seconds. Dogs that pass at the Novice level move on to the next level, the Open/Certificate of Gameness (CG) class. The *Certificate of Gameness (CG)* is awarded to dogs that travel a 30-foot (9.1 m) tunnel with three right angle turns, reaching the quarry within 30 seconds and working it for another minute. In both cases the dog is given only one command from the handler upon release, with no subsequent urging or encouragement.

Half the fun of a terrier trial is watching all the dogs and getting to meet other people who share your love of a fun day with their terrier. Go prepared to spend the day. Get to the trial early but don't try to practice your dog in the tunnels; it's not allowed before the trial. Acclimate your terrier to her surroundings, but don't let her get overheated or tired out. You want her to be comfortable but not bored by the time her turn arrives. Respect the other working terriers during their turns by staying well away and keeping your dog quiet. Do not bring females in season anywhere near the working dogs, or even on the trial grounds. Don't forget to bring food and water and a secure cage in which your dog can rest safely. Staking out is not considered acceptable at a terrier trial.

As you can see, the basics are the same for your Jack no matter what type of earth trial you enter: Go through a tunnel and work a rat, with a few interesting variations on the theme. Be sure to get official rule-books before entering any event. Each association has small rule details that may differ slightly from each other. No matter which association sponsors the trial, or what the exact requirements are, your terrier won't care as long as she is underground putting a rat in its place. Even if you don't care to earn titles on your Jack many owners report that their dogs gain confidence from the experience, although of course very few Jacks have any self-esteem problems to begin with!

## Chapter Ten
# Safe and Sound

For a Jack Russell Terrier, every day is a day of Olympic feats. Your Jack doesn't have to be a sports star to turn every day into a race. With all the running, jumping, climbing, and digging, an active JRT is vulnerable to sports injuries. Most Jacks are pretty tough and will recover with only rest. Some injuries need a little more attention, however, to prevent permanent damage and keep your terrier at the top of his game.

## Dangers Afield

Jack Russell Terriers are never happier than when they are exploring the wilderness. This means that JRT owners, more than most dog owners, need to be savvy about possible dangers in the areas they will be hiking.

### Water Hazards

Even the best swimming dog can't overcome strong surf or undertows, nor can they predict the rogue waves that frequent certain beaches. If a sign says swimming is unsafe for people, it is unsafe for dogs as well. You don't have to be at the ocean to

*The best preventive medicine is caution.*

experience dangerous water. Fast running water in rivers, creeks, and ditches have killed more dogs than rough surf. Some calm mountain streams lead to deadly waterfalls. Normally placid creeks can swell into killer torrents from upstream rain, especially those in desert regions. Many ditches and aqueducts have steep banks or bulkheads that dogs cannot climb. Cold waters pose special hazards. Hypothermic dogs can lose the ability to swim with the strength necessary to make it back to shore. Dogs can break through thin ice. Ice that breaks under a dog's weight will almost certainly not support yours, making rescue dangerous or impossible.

Don't be lulled into complacency simply because your dog is a land-lubber. Shorelines have their own risks. Fish hooks and fishing line can stick in paws, wrap around legs, or be swallowed along with their bait. Sharp shells and rock jetties can gash paws.

A highlight of going to the shore for dogs is the chance to sample all the dead fish. Unfortunately, every year hundreds of dogs in the Northwest get so-called salmon poisoning from eating raw salmon, steelhead, trout, and some other species that are infected with small flukes that in turn contain an organism called *Neorickettsia helminthoeca.* A few days to weeks after eating the infected fish the dog gets progressively sicker. Left untreated, most dogs die within two weeks. If you visit streams or rivers in areas of Northern California, Oregon, Washington, Idaho, or Alaska do not allow your dog to scavenge along the shore.

Don't forget your dog may not be the only animal in the water. The cottonmouth, or water moccasin, lives in swamps, lakes, rivers, and ditches. It often basks on the shore during the day, but is more active at night. It can be identified by light coloration inside its mouth and its way of swim-

ming with its head held out of the water. Its bite can be fatal.

Even more widespread is the snapping turtle. Snappers are aggressive and have bitten body parts off of curious dogs with their sharp beaks. Snappers are found around muddy-bottomed fresh water with abundant plant life, although nesting females can wander far from water. The largest fresh water threat is the alligator. Alligators consider dogs an irresistible delicacy.

The smallest fresh water threat comes from those things in the water you can't even see. Giardia is a microscopic organism found in many water sources; it is nicknamed "beaver-fever" because of its special propensity to be carried by beavers. When your Jack drinks that seemingly pris-

*Water adds a new dimension of fun and an element of danger.*

tine water straight from nature it may ingest giardia and can become ill sometime later with stomach cramps and loose, mucous stools. Giardia is a common condition in dogs that sample wilderness waters, but water doesn't have to be from the wilds to carry microscopic dangers. Pollution, especially in agricultural, industrial, or even residential areas is a common threat. Avoid any water that has a peculiar odor, color, or surface oiliness, or that is obviously fed by run off from polluted areas.

## Land Hazards

Dogs die every year from falling off cliffs or mountainsides. Not only do dogs scamper about with little regard for their safety, but dog paws lack the grasping ability of human hands and once they begin to slip they can do little to stop themselves. To make things worse, mountain and foothill areas may be home to abandoned mine shafts and their air vents.

Although your Jack may think he can best any wild animal, a few animals can get the better of him. Porcupine quills continue to work their way ever deeper into the flesh with every movement. The best way to remove them is with a quick jerk by a pair of pliers, an essential tool in porcupine country. This only applies if you can't get to your veterinarian, who can remove it with less painful techniques. Skunks can make you and your Jack miserable when they are encountered in the open air; their fumes can be potentially deadly when your Jack is underground with one.

Raccoons and badgers avoid dog when they can but can more than hold their own when pushed. A Jack that is enticed into water over its head by a raccoon is in great danger.

The rich assortment of mammal life makes the woodlands a popular area for trapping and hunting. In northern woodlands dogs can be tempted by baits set to entice fur species. Ditches are a favorite site for traps. In farming country poison baits are sometimes left out to get rid of rats.

Poison snakes, and especially rattlesnakes, are high on most people's list of dreaded animals encountered in the wild. With at least 15 separate species, rattlesnakes are found across most of the United States. The preferred habitats vary widely between species, but most prefer drier areas, often retreating in burrows, dense vegetation, hollow logs, or rock outcroppings. Most are primarily nocturnal but may also be active in the daylight during colder months. Rattlesnakes make a characteristic rattling sound as a warning, but unfortunately few dogs are warned off by it. Their venom has proven fatal to many dogs.

The giant marine toad of south Florida (as well as extreme south Texas) is typically four to ten inches long and is primarily nocturnal. It secretes a toxic substance from the large paratoid glands behind its eyes that can burn eyes and sicken dogs, even proving fatal to small dogs and puppies. The gila monster (a type of lizard), found in arid areas under

*Ready for adventure.*

rocks or in burrows, produces a poison from glands along its jaws; their bite could be fatal to a dog the size of Jack Russell Terrier.

Tarantulas, found in the southwestern United States, can inflict a painful bite if provoked. They are nocturnal and hide in crevices during the day, so your dog will probably not run across one. Scorpions, too, are mostly active at night (more so if it rains), hiding under rocks and debris by day. Discourage your Jack from digging and rooting in debris and contact a veterinarian if he is stung.

And one more warning: Although dogs don't get reactions to poison ivy or poison oak, they can carry the irritants on their fur and transmit them to you when you rub it. Keep your dog away from these plants for your own good!

### Inhaled Hazards

Even breathing some air can be dangerous to your dog's health. Valley fever (coccidioidomycosis) is a potentially fatal illness caused by inhaling fungus found in the soil of arid cactus country of the Southwest. This fungus is normally dormant in summer and is killed by freezing temperatures, but it prolifer-

---

### ☆ JACK FACT ☆

**The Real Danger**
Despite a long list of wilderness dangers, the fact remains that most Jacks that are killed are killed by being hit by a car—often in front of their own home. Trust and carelessness can be the most deadly killers of your best friend.

ates after wet weather and can be blown by wind over great distances. Most people and many dogs recover without treatment. But many dogs do not, and need extensive treatment to save their lives.

Blastomycosis comes from fungus in soil and rotting organic debris along the mid-Atlantic seaboard, the north central states, and the Ohio/Mississippi river valley regions. Histoplasmosis fungus is found in the midwestern and eastern states and especially the Mississippi, Missouri, and Ohio River valley regions. It proliferates in bird and bat droppings in moist areas. Both are fatal unless treated aggressively.

Don't deprive your Jack of outdoor adventure, but don't take chances with his safety. Before you unhook the leash, be absolutely certain you know where every road is, every cliff is, where every conceivable danger to your dog is.

# First Aid in the Field

Never go into the field unprepared. Always have a first aid kit available, along with a means of transportation to and communication with an emergency clinic. Follow the directions outlined under the specific emergencies, call ahead to the clinic, and then transport the dog to get professional attention.

### Drowning

Hold the dog upside down by grasping him around his waist and letting his head hang toward the

---

## T E R R I E R   T E C H

### ARTIFICIAL RESPIRATION

1. Open the mouth, clear the passage of secretions and foreign bodies, and pull the tongue forward.
2. Seal your mouth over the dog's nose and mouth. Blow into the dog's nose for two seconds, and then release.
3. If you don't see the chest expand, then blow harder, make a tighter seal around the lips, or check for an obstruction.
4. Repeat at a rate of one breath every four seconds, stopping every minute to monitor breathing and pulse.
5. If air collects in the stomach, push down just behind the rib cage every few minutes.

### CPR

1. Place your hands, one on top of the other, on the left side of the chest about 2 inches up from and behind the point of the elbow.
2. Press down quickly and release.
3. Compress at a rate of about 100 times per minute.
4. After every 15 compressions give two breaths through the nose. If you have a partner, the partner can give breaths every two or three compressions.

worse. Offer small amounts of water for drinking.

You must lower your dog's body temperature quickly, but you don't want the temperature to go below 100°F (37.4°C). Stop cooling the dog when the rectal temperature reaches 103°F (39°C) because it will continue to fall.

Even after the dog seems fully recovered, do not allow him to exert himself for at least three days following the incident. Hyperthermia can cause lasting effects that can result in death unless the dog is fully recovered.

### Hypothermia

An excessively chilled dog will shiver and act sluggish. With continued chilling the body temperature may fall below 95°F (34.7°C), the pulse and breathing rates slow, and the dog may become comatose.

Warm the dog gradually by wrapping it in a blanket that has been warmed in the dryer. Place plastic milk or soda bottles filled with hot water outside the blankets (not touching the dog). You can also place a plastic tarp over the blanket, making sure the dog's head is not covered. Monitor the temperature. Stop warming when the temperature reaches 101°F (37.8°C). Monitor for shock even after the temperature has returned to normal.

### Bleeding

Consider wounds to be an emergency if they bleed profusely, are extremely deep or large, or if they

ground. Let the dog sway back and forth so that water can run out of his mouth. Then administer artificial respiration, with the dog's head positioned lower than his lungs.

### Hyperthermia (Heat Stroke)

Early signs of heat stroke include rapid, loud breathing, abundant thick saliva, bright red mucous membranes, and high rectal temperature. Later signs include unsteadiness, diarrhea, and coma.

Wet the dog down and place him in front of a fan. If this is not possible immerse the dog in cool water. *Do not plunge the dog in ice water;* the resulting constriction of peripheral blood vessels can make the situation open to the chest cavity, abdominal cavity, or head.

• If possible, elevate the wound site, and apply a cold pack to it.

• Do not remove impaled objects; seek veterinary attention.

• Cover the wound with clean dressing and apply pressure. Don't remove blood-soaked bandages; apply more dressings over them until bleeding stops.

• If the wound is on an extremity, apply pressure to the closest pressure point. For a front leg, press inside of the leg just above the elbow; for a rear leg, press inside of the thigh where the femoral artery crosses the thigh bone; for the tail, press the underside of the tail close to where it joins the body.

• Use a tourniquet only in life threatening situations and only when all other attempts have failed. Check for signs of shock.

• For abdominal wounds, place a warm wet sterile dressing over any protruding internal organs and cover with a bandage or towel. Do not attempt to push organs back into the dog.

• For head wounds, apply gentle pressure to control bleeding. Monitor for loss of consciousness or shock and treat accordingly.

• For animal bites, allow some bleeding, then clean the area thoroughly and apply antibiotic ointment. A course of oral antibiotics will probably be necessary. It's best not to suture most animal bites, but a large one (over one half inch in diameter), or one on the face or other prominent position, may need to be sutured.

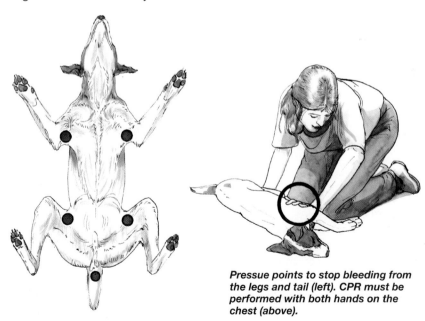

*Pressue points to stop bleeding from the legs and tail (left). CPR must be performed with both hands on the chest (above).*

## Limb Fractures

Lameness associated with extreme pain, swelling or deformation of the affected leg, or grinding or popping sounds could indicate a break or another serious problem. Attempts to immobilize fractures with splints tend to do more harm than good, so it's best to keep the dog still and cushion the limb from further trauma without splinting if you can get to the veterinarian right away.

## Snakebites

Poisonous snakebites are characterized by swelling, discoloration, pain, fangmarks, restlessness, nausea, and weakness. Most bites are to the head, and are difficult to treat with first aid. The best first aid is to keep the dog quiet and take it to the veterinarian immediately. Antivenin is the treatment of choice.

## Insect Stings and Allergic Reactions

Insects often sting dogs on the face or feet. Remove any visible stingers as quickly as possible by brushing them with a credit card or stiff paper; grasping a stinger often injects more venom into the dog. Administer baking soda and water paste to bee stings, and vinegar to wasp stings. Clean the area and apply antibacterial ointment.

Call your veterinarian immediately if you think the dog may be having a severe reaction. Insect stings are the most common cause of extreme allergic reactions in dogs. Swelling around the nose and throat can block the airway. Other possible reactions include restlessness, vomiting, diarrhea, seizures, and collapse. If any of these symptoms occur, immediate veterinary attention will probably be necessary.

# Nonemergency Injuries

More often, the injuries sustained in the field will be minor. Some, however, can ultimately be just as serious if they aren't treated.

## Foxtails

Foxtails are barbed seeds that can cause serious problems to dogs. Once embedded in or inhaled by a dog the seed's barbs allow it to migrate through the dog's body, sometimes causing abscesses and sometimes even entering vital organs. Symptoms include localized infections or apparent pain, irritation to the nose, eyes, or ears, and strange behaviors involving rubbing and licking parts of the dog's own body. The most common site of migration is the external ear canal, involving about half of all cases. Other common sites include the webbing between the toes, eye, nose, lumbar area, and thoracic cavity. Foxtails usually have to be removed under anesthesia.

### Foot Injuries

Burrs, cuts, peeled pads, broken nails, or other foot injuries can cause lameness. Cuts and peeled pads should be carefully flushed with warm water, and an antibacterial ointment applied. Cover the area with gauze, then wrap the foot with a bandage such as Vet-Wrap (a stretchable bandage that clings to itself). You can also add padding. Change the dressing twice daily (or anytime it gets wet) and restrict exercise until it heals.

If you need a quick fix for a minor injury, you can fashion a makeshift pad by adhering a thin piece of rubber or leather to the bottom of the pad with super glue, or you can apply a coat of Nu-Skin (available at drug stores) if the injury is not too extensive. Peeled pads are very painful. A local anesthetic such as hemorrhoid cream or a topical toothache salve can help ease some

*Prompt medical attention can prevent life-long problems.*

of the discomfort. Deep cuts or extensive peeling should be checked by your veterinarian for foreign objects or tendon damage.

A split nail can be treated by cutting it as short as possible and soaking it in warm salt water. Apply an antibiotic and then a human fingernail mender, followed by a bandage.

If a toe is swollen, does not match its fellow on the opposite foot in

---

### ☆ JACK FACT ☆

**Check for Dehydration**
To check your dog's hydration, pick up the skin on the back just above the shoulders, so that it makes a slight tent above the body. It should pop back into place almost immediately. If it remains tented and separated from the body, your dog is dehydrated.

## JOINT PROBLEMS

Joints occur at the moving junction of two bones. The ends of the bones are covered with cartilage, which helps to cushion impact and allows for smoother movement between the bones. The joint is enclosed by the joint capsule, the inner layer of which is the synovial membrane. The synovial membrane produces synovial fluid, a thick liquid that fills the joint cavity and provides lubrication and nourishment. Cartilage can be injured from excessive joint stress or from any preexisting joint instability allowing the bones to bump together abnormally. Injured cartilage releases enzymes that break down the normally thick synovial fluid into a thin fluid that neither lubricates nor nourishes adequately, in turn resulting in further cartilage deterioration. If the dog continues to stress the joint, damage will increase until it extends to the joint capsule and bone. Only at this point are sensory nerves affected so that the dog feels pain. This means that considerable joint damage has already been done by the time your dog exhibits lameness from a preexisting condition.

**Synovitis:** Active dogs can subject their joints to excessive forces, stretching the joint capsule and inflaming the surrounding soft tissue. Small blood vessels in the tissue dilate and the vessel walls leak fluid into the joint cavity. This influx of excess fluid causes swelling and pain, a condition recognized as synovitis. Continued synovitis leads to an inflammatory response that damages the articular cartilage and its ability to act as a shock absorber. Eventually the loss of cushioning can lead to irreparable damage to the bony component of the joint.

**Arthritis:** In older dogs, or dogs with a previous injury, limping is often the result of degenerative joint disease (DJD)—more commonly called arthritis. In some dogs there is no obvious cause. In others abnormal stresses or trauma to the joint can cause degeneration of the joint cartilage and underlying bone. The synovial membrane surrounding the joint becomes inflamed and the bone develops small bony outgrowths called osteophytes. These changes cause the joint to stiffen, become painful, and have decreased range of motion. In cases in which an existing condition is exacerbating the DJD, surgery to remedy the condition is warranted.

When considering surgery for a joint problem, keep in mind that the more the joint is used in its damaged state, the more DJD will occur. Even though the surgery may fix the initial problem, if too much damage has occurred the dog will still be plagued with incurable arthritic changes. Prevention of arthritis is the key.

Conservative treatment entails keeping the dog's weight down, attending to injuries, and maintaining a program of exercise. Low impact exercise such as walking or swimming every other day is best for dogs with signs of arthritis. Newer drugs, such as carprofen, are available from your veterinarian and may help alleviate some of the symptoms of DJD, but they should be used only with careful veterinary supervision. Some newer drugs

## *JOINT PROBLEMS (continued)*

and supplements may actually improve the joint. Polysulfated glycosaminoglycan increases the compressive resilience of cartilage. Glucosamine stimulates the synthesis of collagen, and may help rejuvenate cartilage to some extent. Chondroitin sulfate helps to shield cartilage from destructive enzymes.

**Ruptured Cruciate Ligament:** Ligaments provide stability to joints by connecting one bone to another. They are made of dense connective tissue that becomes less elastic with age; when stretched by more than about 10 percent, tearing occurs. The anterior cruciate ligament prevents the stifle joint from slipping from side to side. Injuries occur most often during jump-ing or acceleration, or from a strong sideways force, especially in obese dogs. Because most cruciate tears don't get well on their own they usually require surgery, even if they are only partial tears. The instability in the stifle caused by the torn cruciate ligament causes further damage to the surrounding medial meniscus (which may or may not have also torn with the initial injury). This torn meniscus often produces a clicking noise when the dog is walking or trotting. Without stabilization degenerative changes will cause the joint to become arthritic. Several methods of surgical repair are in use, and even newer cruciate repair techniques may hold promise; consult a veterinarian familiar with orthopedic surgeries.

*Five minutes a week checking your dog's health can add years to his life.*

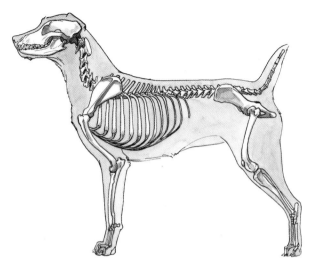

*Skeletal structure of the JRT.*

# Lameness Therapies

Complete rest and total inactivity are the best initial home care for any lameness. Rest your dog well past the time it quits limping. A veterinarian should examine any extreme lameness, or any slight lameness that persists without significant improvement after three days of complete rest. Exercise therapy is equally as important, but exercise must be controlled. Leash walking and swimming are excellent low impact exercises for recovering dogs.

shape and position, makes a grinding sound when moved, or if the dog is in considerable pain, the dog should be kept quiet and checked by your veterinarian. Meanwhile minimize swelling by applying cold packs or placing the foot in a bucket of cold water.

In many injuries in which the limb must be rested passive motion can be important in preventing muscle contraction and maintaining the health of the joint. All movements should be slow and well within the joint's normal range of motion. Massage therapy can be useful for loosening tendons and increasing circulation.

Many injuries are quite painful and may require drug therapy for pain relief. Orthopedic surgeries can be particularly painful and almost always warrant analgesics. Pain has a self-perpetuating aspect, which means that it is easier to prevent than to stop. Discuss with your veterinarian the pros and cons of various analgesics.

Ice packs may help minimize swelling if applied immediately after an injury. The reduced tissue temperature lowers the metabolic rate and inhibits edema and the sensa-

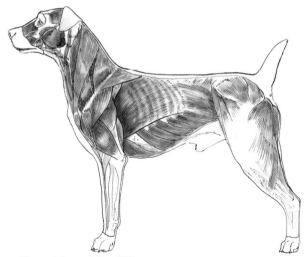

*Musculature of the JRT.*

tion of pain. Cold therapy can be helpful for up to a week following an injury.

Heat therapy can be beneficial to older injuries. Heat increases the metabolic rate of the tissue, relaxes muscle spasms, and can provide some pain relief. Moist heat applied for about 20-minute periods is preferable, and care must be taken to avoid burning. Other types of heat therapy are available that penetrate more deeply through the tissues, but because they also carry a greater risk of burn injury they should only be performed by an experienced person.

# The Five-Minute Checkup

Even if you don't have a sports star, the best five minutes you can spend with your dog every week is performing a quick health check. You'll be getting to know how your dog looks when he's healthy, you'll get a head start on any problems, and your dog will think you just can't resist petting him all over.

Check:
• the mouth for red, bleeding, swollen or pale gums, loose teeth, ulcers of the tongue or gums, or bad breath
• the eyes for discharge, cloudiness, or discolored "whites"
• the ears for foul odor, redness, discharge, or crusted tips
• the nose for thickened or colored discharge

• the skin for parasites, hair loss, crusts, red spots, or lumps
• the feet for cuts, abrasions, split nails, bumps, or misalligned toes
• the anal region for redness, swelling, or discharge

Watch your dog for signs of lameness or incoordination, sore neck, circling, loss of muscling, and for any behavioral change. Run your hands over the muscles and bones and check that they are symmetrical from one side to the other. Weigh your dog and observe whether he is gaining or losing. Check for any growths, swellings, sores, or pigmented lumps. Look out for mammary masses, changes in testicle size, discharge from the vulva or penis, increased or decreased urination, foul smelling or strangely colored urine, incontinence, swollen abdomen, black or bloody stool, change in appetite or water consumption, difficulty breathing, lethargy, coughing, gagging, or loss of balance.

# Normal Values

Understanding the normal values for your dog will help you detect when something isn't right.

### Gum Color

The simplest yet most overlooked checkpoint is your dog's gum color. Looking at the gums is so simple, yet virtually no one does it—except your veterinarian, who will look at the gums before anything else when

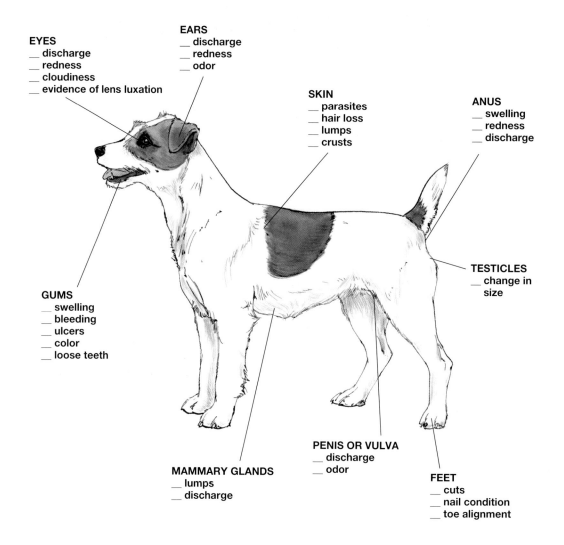

**EYES**
__ discharge
__ redness
__ cloudiness
__ evidence of lens luxation

**EARS**
__ discharge
__ redness
__ odor

**SKIN**
__ parasites
__ hair loss
__ lumps
__ crusts

**ANUS**
__ swelling
__ redness
__ discharge

**TESTICLES**
__ change in size

**GUMS**
__ swelling
__ bleeding
__ ulcers
__ color
__ loose teeth

**MAMMARY GLANDS**
__ lumps
__ discharge

**PENIS OR VULVA**
__ discharge
__ odor

**FEET**
__ cuts
__ nail condition
__ toe alignment

*External health checklist.*

your dog comes into the exam room sick.
• Normal gum color is a good deep pink.
• Pale gum color can indicate anemia or poor circulation.

• White or very light gum color can indicate shock, severe anemia, or very poor circulation.
• Bluish gum or tongue color indicates imminent life-threatening lack of oxygen.

## *BLOOD TESTS*

*CBC reports:*
• Red blood cells: the cells responsible for carrying oxygen throughout the body
• White blood cells: the infection fighting cells
• Platelets: components responsible for clotting blood to stop bleeding

*Blood Chemistry Test reports:*
• Albumin (ALB): reduced levels are suggestive of liver or kidney disease, or parasites
• Alanine aminotransferase (ALT): elevated levels suggest liver disease
• Alkaline phosphatase (ALKP): elevated levels can indicate liver disease or Cushing's syndrome
• Amylase (AMYL): elevated levels suggest pancreatic or kidney disease

• Blood urea nitrogen (BUN): elevated levels suggest kidney disease
• Calcium (CA): elevated levels suggest kidney or parathyroid disease or some types of tumors
• Cholesterol (CHOL): elevated levels suggest liver or kidney disease or several other disorders
• Creatinine (CREA): elevated levels suggest kidney disease or urinary obstruction
• Blood Glucose (GLU): low levels can suggest liver disease
• Phosphorous (PHOS): elevated levels can suggest kidney disease
• Total bilirubin (TBIL): level can indicate problems in the bile ducts
• Total protein (TP): level can indicate problems of the liver, kidney, or gastrointestinal tract.

**Blood tests provide a window to the internal organs.**

*Always keep an eye out for signs of abnormal movement or loss of strength or coordination.*

- Bright red gum color can indicate carbon monoxide poisoning.
- Yellowish color can indicate jaundice.
- Little tiny red splotches (called petechia) can indicate a blood clotting problem.

Don't confuse a red line around the gum line with healthy gums. A dog with dirty teeth can have gum disease, giving an unhealthy, but rosy, glow to the gums, especially at the margins around the teeth.

Besides color, capillary refill time, which is an index of blood circulation, can be estimated simply by pressing on the gum with your finger and lifting your finger off. The gum where you pressed will be momentarily white, but will quickly re-pink as the blood moves back into the area. If it takes longer than a couple of seconds to re-pink, circulation is poor.

## Body Temperature

Your dog's body temperature is another clue about what's going on inside. As in humans, temperature will be slightly lower in the morning and higher in the evening. Normal temperature for a Jack Russell is about 100 to 102°F (37.4–38.5°C). If the temperature is:
- 103°F (39.1°C) or above, call the veterinarian and ask for advice.
- 105°F (40.2°C) or above, go to the emergency clinic. A temperature of 106°F (41°C) and above is dangerous.

- 98°F (36.3°C) or below, call the veterinarian.
- 96°F (35.2°C) or below, go to the emergency clinic.

## Pulse

The easiest way to check your dog's pulse is to feel the pulse through the femoral artery. If your dog is standing, cup your hand around the top of his leg and feel around the inside of it, almost where it joins with the torso. If your dog is on his back, you can sometimes even see the pulse in this area. Normal pulse rate for a Jack Russell at rest is about 60 to 120 beats per minute.

You can feel your dog's heartbeat by placing your hand on his lower rib cage just behind his elbow. Don't be alarmed if it seems irregular; the heartbeat of many dogs is irregular compared to humans. Have your veterinarian check it out, then get used to how it feels when it is normal.

## Blood Tests

Your Jack's blood can provide valuable clues about his state of health. Blood tests are vital before your pet undergoes surgery to ensure that he is healthy enough for the procedure. The most common tests are the Complete Blood Count (CBC) and the Blood Chemistry Test ("Chem panel"). Many other specialized tests are fairly common.

# Chapter Eleven
# Heredity and Health

There's no such thing as a dog—purebred or mixed—that doesn't carry some recessive deleterious genes in its makeup. These usually cause no problems, even for generations, until by chance, a mating occurs between two dogs carrying the same deleterious gene. The smaller the gene pool from which a breed originated, the more likely such a chance meeting will happen, because it's inevitable that some of the founding ancestors of the breed would carry and pass on its particular detrimental genes. Despite the historically open criteria for recognition as a Jack Russell Terrier, the breed still has a limited gene pool that descends from relatively few ancestral foundation dogs.

Careless breeding increases the incidence of hereditary problems, but even carefully bred dogs can be affected. Jack Russell Terriers are extremely healthy compared to other pure breeds, but even they carry a hereditary burden that includes a couple of major problems and several minor ones.

*Jacks are generally healthy—but nobody's perfect.*

# Neural

Disorders of the nervous system, including the brain, spinal cord, nerve cells, and the chemicals (called neurotransmitters) that influence them, can result in degrees of impairment ranging from mild to deadly.

## Deafness
The most common cause of deafness in young dogs is hereditary pigment related deafness, such as that associated with genes responsible for lack of pigmentation in the coat, iris of the eye, and other body parts. One of the most prominent of these genes is the extreme piebald ($s^w$) allele, which is found in predominantly white JRT's. Dogs can be either deaf in one ear or both; partial deafness within one ear is not seen. The inheritance is not straightforward: Offspring of normally hearing parents can be deaf, and offspring of bilaterally deaf parents can have normal hearing. In general, however, deaf dogs are more likely to produce deaf dogs than non-deaf dogs are.

The association with coat color is more than just coincidental; animals with alleles that result not only in absence of coat pigmentation but in missing pigment on other body structures may also be lacking normal pigment on some internal body structures. For example, normal blood vessels have pigment-producing cells (called melanocytes) within them that seem to be important for normal development. Dogs with the $s^w$ alleles apparently have melanocyte-deficient blood vessels leading to the inner ear. Affected dogs are born with normal auditory structures, but soon after birth these blood vessels degenerate. Parts of the inner ear, including the hair cells responsible for hearing, subsequently degenerate, so that these dogs are deaf by about one month of age.

**Diagnosis:** In dogs with normal hearing, the auditory signals travel from the ear to the brain by way of

*Check your Jack's hearing by watching his reaction to noises from hidden sources.*

the brainstem. The Brainstem Auditory Evoked Response (BAER) records electrical activity of the brainstem in response to sounds, and can indicate whether a dog's ear is functioning normally. This test is painless and is conducted in awake dogs. Because deafness in the JRT is present by two to three weeks of age, all puppies should be BAER tested before going to their new homes. Responsible breeders should test their breeding stock and decline to breed deaf dogs.

Although some preliminary screening tests can be done in the home, the results may not be very accurate, and they can only detect dogs with bilateral deafness. Saying a word to which the dog normally responds when the dog's attention is elsewhere and when the dog cannot see the person speaking is a simple preliminary test. Ringing a bell or making an unusual sound from behind the dog should result in either the dog's attention (as shown by head turning or ear twitching) or a startle reaction. Dogs that are panting will usually stop panting momentarily in order to listen, so this can be used as a tentative sign of hearing. Testers must be careful that no wind currents from clapping hands or vibrations through the floor reach the dog, and that the dog cannot see the tester out of the corner of its eye (bearing in mind that dogs have a greater peripheral field of vision than humans) and cannot see the tester's shadow or reflection. Other dogs that could provide cues by their response should be removed from the area. Dogs habituate to sounds rapidly; repeating the test will often result in lack of responsiveness. These tests can generally detect a dog that is deaf in both ears. A dog that is deaf in one ear will still respond to words and sounds in a manner almost indistinguishable from a dog with normal hearing.

**Prognosis:** Unilaterally deaf dogs make excellent companions and their owners often are never aware that the dog has any loss of hearing. Bilaterally deaf dogs present a more challenging, and controversial, situation. These dogs are at greater risk of being killed or injured in an accident because they cannot hear their owners calls or cannot hear approaching danger. They may be more prone to snap because they can be easily startled by the sudden appearance of a dog or person, although the tendency to snap is highly dependent on the dog's temperament. Deaf dogs can be difficult to train because special ways of first having the dog watch the owner must be taught, and then visual or tactile signals must be utilized. Owners who do not realize their dog is deaf too often conclude it is stupid or stubborn and may abuse or abandon it. Many people have raised deaf dogs successfully, however. They employ hand signals, flashlights, vibrating collars, and even other dogs to help them communicate with their deaf pets. Nonetheless, living with a totally deaf dog presents hardships not encountered when living with a dog that can hear.

---

★ **JACK FACT** ★

**On Deaf Ears**
Owners of deaf dogs can find advice through several sources:

Website: Deafness in Dogs and Cats: *http://www.lsu.edu/guests/senate/public_html/deaf.htm*

Book: Cope-Becker S. *Living With a Deaf Dog: A Book of Advice, Facts and Experiences About Canine Deafness*. Cincinnatti: Self-published. 1997.

---

## Ataxia

Nerve impulses travel from one nerve cell, or neuron, to another by way of long segments (called axons), which are often covered with a fatty insulating substance called myelin. When myelin is lost, as it is in some diseases, it slows the nerve impulses. In some JRT's, myelin is lost in the neurons of the spinal cord. These same dogs may also have neuronal degeneration in parts of the brain and auditory pathways. The initial symptom (which can occur as early as two to four months of age) is incoordination of the rear legs. The condition gradually worsens over months to years until all four legs are affected and the dog may lose the ability to walk. No treatment is available. The mode of inheritance in JRT's is unknown; however, Smooth Fox Terriers have a similar disorder that is inherited in a manner consistent with a single recessive gene. At this time it is unknown if it is the same disorder as that in the JRT.

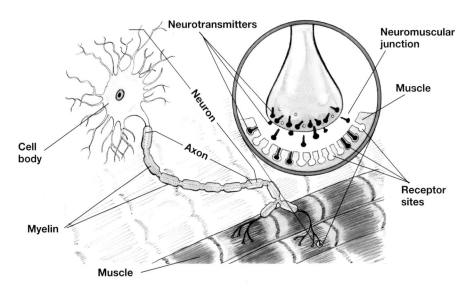

Neurotransmitters

Neuromuscular junction

Muscle

Cell body

Neuron

Axon

Receptor sites

Myelin

Muscle

## Myasthenia Gravis

In normal dogs, a nerve impulse causes a muscle to contract by releasing a particular chemical (in this case, acetylcholine) that travels over a small gap between the nerve cell and the muscle (called the neuromuscular junction). When the chemical reaches the muscle, it stimulates it by being taken up by places called receptor sites. Dogs with myasthenia gravis (MG) don't have enough receptor sites, so the muscles are not stimulated as they should be. This causes muscle weakness, especially after sustained activity. The dog regains its strength when allowed to rest.

Both a congenital form and an acquired form of MG exists in dogs. JRT's have an increased risk for the congenital form, which appears to be inherited as a single autosomal recessive allele. These dogs begin to exhibit symptoms by three to eight

weeks of age. As they tire with exercise, the gait becomes choppy and the dog finally stops and rests. Regurgitation, salivation, and pupil dilation are additional symptoms. The most convincing diagnostic test is to give the dog a drug (edrophomium chloride) that allows the neurotransmitter chemical to remain available to the muscle receptors for a longer time, but this test should only be given by veterinarians familiar with its use and possible side effects.

Affected JRT's are prone to aspiration pneumonia (pneumonia from breathing in fluids), which can be fatal, and to megaesophagus (enlarged esophagus), which causes the dog to regurgitate food. Screening and treatment for pneumonia is important for affected dogs; feeding them from a raised platform can help the food travel to the stomach. MG can be treated by administering a long acting drug that increases the time acetylcholine persists in the neuromuscular junction, but long-term results with puppies are at best uncertain.

## Jack Russell Terrier Neuroaxonal Dystrophy

Neuroaxonal dystrophy is a group of disorders in which a metabolic error causes swellings (called spheroids) along a region of the neurons' axons. In JRT neuroaxonal dystrophy, extensive neuronal swelling occurs, especially in the brainstem (the part of the brain that controls many basic body functions, including breathing and heart contractions).

## Seizure Disorders

Seizures are not uncommon in dogs, and may or may not have hereditary causes. Many environmental factors can contribute to seizures, and often the cause is never determined. Epilepsy is usually diagnosed when a dog, especially a young dog, has repeated seizures for no apparent reason. Such dogs very likely have a hereditary form of epilepsy.

Seizures typically begin with the dog acting nervous and then exhibiting increasingly peculiar behaviors (such as trembling, unresponsiveness, staring into space, and salivating profusely). This "pre-ictal" stage is followed by the ictal stage, in which the dog will typically stiffen, fall over, and paddle its legs and champ its jaws; the dog may also urinate, defecate, salivate, and vocalize. During this time the dog should be protected from injuries caused by hitting furniture or falling down stairs (wrapping it in a blanket can help secure it), and from other dogs (dogs will often attack a convulsing dog). The ictal stage usually lasts only a couple of minutes; if it continues for more than 10 minutes the dog should be taken to an emergency clinic. After the ictal stage, the dog will remain disoriented, may be blind, and will pant and sleep. This post-ictal stage may last from minutes to days. A veterinary exam of the dog, including a complete history and description of the seizure onset and activity, should be performed as soon as possible.

**Diagnosis:** No specific tests are available to confirm a diagnosis of epilepsy, although some abnormalities in the chemical composition of cerebrospinal fluid have been identified in some epileptic dogs.

Dogs with recurrent seizures can be treated with the drug phenobarbitol, which is usually effective in preventing seizures. Another drug, potassium bromide, can also be prescribed if results are not satisfactory with phenobarbitol.

Because epilepsy is found more often in some breeds than others, and often runs in families, it is

---

★ **JACK FACT** ★

**Epilepsy**
For more information on epilepsy visit the Canine Epilepsy Resource Center at *http://www.rt66.com/~dalcrazy/Epil-K9.html*

---

believed to have a hereditary component. In the breeds in which it has been studied most comprehensively, epilepsy appears to be inherited in a mode consistent with a single recessive allele. Other evidence points to the probability that different genes cause epilepsy in different breeds, a situation that will delay a DNA test for it in all breeds.

# Ocular

The eye is a complex structure prone to various types of disorders involving the lids, the various layers of the eye, or the neural components involved in vision. Their effects can range from mild irritation to severe pain and blindness.

## Lens Luxation

The lens is normally held in position by a ring of tiny suspensory fibers called zonules. Trauma to the eye can damage the fibers, and in some dogs the zonules are inherently weak and prone to rupture. If only some of the fibers break, the lens may be only partially displaced, in which case the condition is known as subluxation of the lens. If enough fibers break, the lens floats out of position (a condition called luxation of the lens), sometimes through the pupil into the front of the eye. When this happens it can cut off the normal drainage of the eye's aqueous humor and cause secondary glaucoma (see page 158), or it can cause corneal edema if it comes into contact with the inner surface of the cornea.

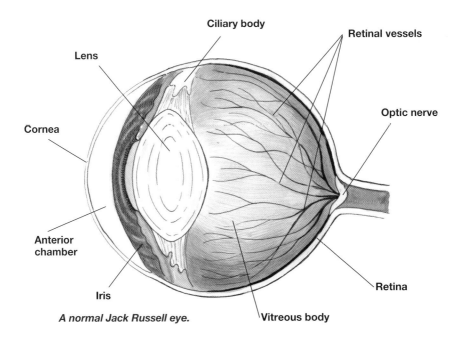

*A normal Jack Russell eye.*

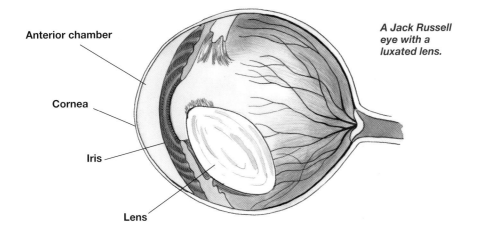

Anterior chamber

Cornea

Iris

Lens

*A Jack Russell eye with a luxated lens.*

**Diagnosis:** Symptoms of lens luxation vary according to its severity and secondary effects. They can include redness, squinting, pain, corneal cloudiness, and even the observation of the lens in the front of the iris or the edge of the lens through the pupil.

**Prognosis:** No prevention is available. Treatment of mild cases involves controlling intraocular pressure and administration of eye medications, but most cases require removal of the lens. A dog without a lens can still see, but images are in extremely poor focus. Replacing the lens with an artificial lens can restore the optical system of the eye so that the dog can see images in sharp focus.

Dogs in which lens subluxation or luxation occurs for no apparent reason are considered to have a hereditary predisposition to the disorder,

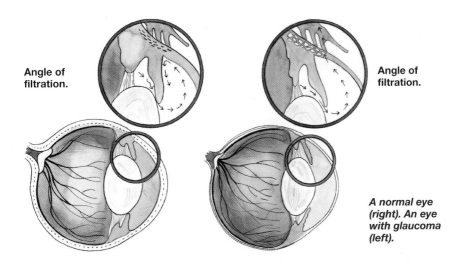

Angle of filtration.

Angle of filtration.

*A normal eye (right). An eye with glaucoma (left).*

but the genetic nature is not known at this time. Although only one eye may be initially involved, in these dogs both eyes are usually ultimately affected. The typical age of onset ranges from two to seven years, most commonly four or five years of age.

## Glaucoma

The eye constantly produces aqueous fluid, which fills the area between the lens and the cornea, providing nutrients to these structures. The fluid must be drained from the chamber at the same rate it is produced; drainage is through structures at the junction of the iris and cornea. If fluid production exceeds drainage, then the intraocular pressure (IOP) will rise.

*The eyes are the windows to the soul— keep them clear.*

Anything that interferes with normal drainage can cause glaucoma. Sometimes a luxated lens falls into a position that blocks the drainage, or the eye is injured or inflamed such that the drainage is compromised; such cases of glaucoma are called secondary glaucoma. Cases in which glaucoma does not arise from trauma or other disease are termed primary glaucoma and are considered to be hereditary.

Glaucoma usually occurs in only one eye at a time. Outward symptoms include an eye that is painful,

*Hereditary eye problems are seldom evident in puppies.*

reddened, and swollen, with a clouded cornea and dilated pupil. The dog may rub its eye and squint. These symptoms are especially apparent when the rise in IOP is sudden. If the pressure isn't lowered quickly, permanent damage to the eye and blindness will result. When IOP is higher than blood pressure in the arteries, then it prevents blood from entering the vessels within the eye, depriving the retina of oxygen and nutrients, ultimately leading to cell death and blindness. Other structures within the eye are also irrevocably damaged. For this reason, and because of the pain associated with it, glaucoma is a medical emergency. Medications or surgery can help in some cases, but even with the best and swiftest of care often vision cannot be saved. In these cases it is usually best to remove the blind eye so that the glaucoma cannot continue to cause pain to the dog.

## Cataracts

The lens lies behind the pupil and iris of the eye and focuses the light on the retina. Many dogs get cataracts (opacities of the lens) as they age, or as a result of trauma or other disease. In some JRT's cataracts can appear at a young age, usually before age seven years. These cataracts, termed juvenile cataracts, are usually hereditary. In severe cases, the lens can be removed and replaced with a prosthetic lens.

*Jack Russell Terriers, whether short-legged or long-legged, do everything at full throttle.*

### Distichiasis

In distichiasis, abnormally positioned eyelashes project toward the eye from either lid, touching the cornea. This can cause considerable discomfort, and damage to the cornea. The reddened eye may have a discharge, and the cornea may develop a dull or bluish colored area. In the worst cases, the irritation can lead to infection and blindness. Plucking the abnormal hairs is usually only a temporary measure. Surgical removal or electroepilation, among other techniques, usually provides permanent relief. Distichiasis is believed to have a hereditary basis; some researchers believe it is inherited as a single dominant trait.

### Other Disorders

Other ocular disorders with a possible hereditary basis that have been reported in Jack Russell Terriers include:

**Microphthalmia:** Abnormally small globe of the eye.

**Persistent pupillary membrane:** Strands of tissue spanning the pupil, or sometimes spanning the area between the cornea and pupil, that are remnants of the blood supply to the fetal eye.

## Skeletal

Disorders of the bones and joints are among the most common hereditary disorders in dogs. Heavy breeds are more likely to suffer from hip and elbow dysplasia, whereas small breeds are more likely to suffer from Legg-Calve'-Perthes disease or patellar luxation. It is these latter problems that are more often seen in JRT's.

## Legg-Calvé-Perthes Disease

Legg-Calvé-Perthes disease (LCPD—also known as Legg-Perthes or avascular (or aseptic) necrosis of the femoral head) is a condition in which normal blood supply to the head of the femur (thigh) bone is decreased, resulting in degeneration of the bone. The femoral head weakens and may collapse, resulting in degenerative joint disease and poor hip function. LCPD occurs most often in young dogs of small breeds, often beginning subtly at three to four months of age. Once the femoral head collapses, the joint becomes quite painful and the dog will be lame on that leg. In most cases only one leg is affected.

Radiographs (X rays) can detect early changes and allow for some preventive measures. Complete and absolute rest of the joint for four to six months can prevent permanent damage, but this route is impractical with a JRT puppy. Placing the leg in a sling has been suggested, but it causes its own set of permanent problems and is no longer recommended. At present the preferred treatment is surgical removal of the affected femoral head, followed by physical therapy for several weeks. In small dogs the muscles are able to hold the joint together adequately even without a femoral head.

A hereditary component is suspected. The best model at present is a single recessive allele with incomplete penetrance. The Institute for Genetic Disease Control in Animals maintains a registry open to JRT's in which pedigrees of dogs clear from LCPD can be found.

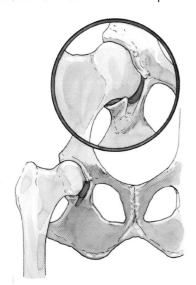 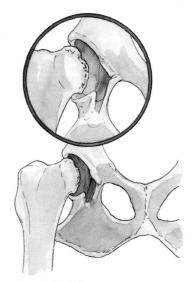

*A normal hip (left). A hip with necrosis of the femoral neck (right).*

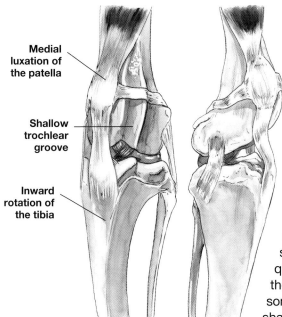

Medial luxation of the patella

Shallow trochlear groove

Inward rotation of the tibia

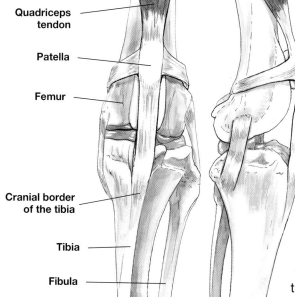

Quadriceps tendon

Patella

Femur

Cranial border of the tibia

Tibia

Fibula

*A stifle with patellar luxation (top).*
*A normal stifle (bottom). Front views on*
*left. Side views on right.*

## Patellar Luxation

The dog's stifle is the joint analogous to the human knee, connecting the femur (thigh) bone to the tibia and fibula (shin) bones. The stifle joint also contains three smaller bones, including the patella (kneecap). The patella's inner surface normally glides up and down within the trochlear groove of the femur as the knee flexes and contracts. It is also secured by the tendon of the quadraceps muscle as well as the surrounding joint capsule. In some dogs the groove may be too shallow, or the quadraceps exert too much pull, causing the patella to occasionally pop out of place (luxate) when the knee is moving. When this happens the dogs usually holds the leg up and hops for a few steps, perhaps even yelping in pain. Depending on the severity of the condition, the patella may pop back into place on its own. Four grades of patellar luxation severity are described:

• **Grade 1:** The dog occasionally skips, holding one hind leg forward for a step or two. The patella can be manually shifted in and out of position.

• **Grade 2:** The dog usually holds the affected leg up, only occasionally bearing weight on it. When the leg is manipulated it has a grinding feeling.

*Healthy limbs make playful and happy Jacks.*

• **Grade 3:** The patella is permanently out of position, although the dog will still sometimes stand on the leg.

• **Grade 4:** The patella is always out of position and the dog never puts its weight on the leg.

Patellar luxation can occur in one (unilaterally) or both (bilaterally) hind legs, and the patella can be displaced toward the inside (medially) or outside (laterally) of the joint. In affected JRT's, it is almost always displaced medially. A dog with bilateral medially luxated patellas will have a bow-legged appearance when standing. Medial luxation is usually present by four to six months of age, although the symptoms may go unnoticed for years. Each time the patella pops out of position it stretches the surrounding tissues that are needed to hold it in place, eventually even wearing down the edge of the trochlear groove, so that the condition gradually worsens. This deterioration may possibly be forestalled by keeping the dog at a trim weight, building its muscles with steady, moderate exercise (such as walking and swimming), and attempting to keep the cartilage healthy with glucosamine supplementation. Surgery in which the soft tissue surrounding the patella is reconstructed can yield excellent results when done at these early stages.

Grades 3 and 4 luxation are quite painful and require surgery for relief. The type of surgery will depend upon the particular dog's condition and the cause of the problem, but usually it entails tightening and suturing any stretched tissues. In addition, if the groove is shallow or worn flat it may need to be reconstructed. If the quadraceps muscle is pulling on the patella and causing it to luxate it may need to be realigned. Even after surgery the stifle may not be operating perfectly, but it will be much improved. This improvement is much more likely if the surgery is performed by a veterinarian who is experienced in orthopedic surgery.

## Radial Agenesis and Premature Closure of the Ulna

During development the long bones of the forelegs (the radius and ulna) must develop at the same rate and to the same extent for normal orientation of the front limbs. If the radius is abnormally shorter than the ulna (a condition called radial agenesis) the front legs will appear bowed. If the ulna stops growing before the radius (a condition called premature closure of the ulna) the feet will turn out.

## Short or "High" Toes

In some JRT's the outside toes of the front feet are abnormally short, such that they don't touch the ground when the dog is standing normally. This doesn't cause any problems for most dogs but is not normal structure.

## Malocclusions

The normal JRT occlusion ("bite") is a scissors bite, in which the teeth of the upper jaw are positioned immediately in front of the teeth of the lower jaw. Small deviations from the ideal bite usually are of little medical consequence. Larger deviations may or may not have adverse affects

on the dog. An overshot bite occurs when the lower jaw is significantly shorter than the upper jaw. In severe cases the lower canine teeth are situated behind the upper canine teeth, and the molars may oppose each other rather than interdigitate. An undershot bite occurs when the lower jaw is longer than the upper jaw. A wry mouth is the situation when only one side of the jaw is undershot or overshot. Most occlusion problems are considered to have a hereditary basis, but the genetic nature is unknown.

Missing teeth are a common occurrence in most breeds; most often the small premolars are missing. In some breeds (including the Fox Terrier), the trait is inherited in a manner consistent with a single recessive gene, and it is not unlikely that the JRT shares this pattern of inheritance.

# Circulatory

Compared to most breeds, JRT's have healthy circulatory systems, but they, too, have their baggage. All dogs should be screened by having a veterinarian listen to the heart for a murmur. Heart murmurs indicate a turbulent blood flow, usually the result of blood being forced through too small an opening. They are usually graded from I to VI in severity, with VI being worst. Dogs with murmurs (especially those above grade II) should be seen by a veterinary cardiologist for an ultrasound of the heart.

*Ready for the next adventure life serves up.*

## Cardiomyopathy

Dilated Cardiomyopathy (DCM) is a progressive disease in which the muscles of the heart lose their contractility. The heart compensates by several mechanisms that ultimately produce an enlarged heart with thin muscle walls. Symptoms include coughing, labored or rapid breathing, weight loss, general debilitation, abdominal distention, cold extremities, fainting episodes, and heart murmur. Definitive diagnosis is with an electrocardiogram and ultrasound. In most breeds, there is no prevention and no cure for cardiomyopathy, and dogs eventually die of congestive heart failure or severe arrythmias (abnormal beating).

## Patent Ductus Arteriosis

During fetal life the lungs are not functional, so a vessel (the ductus arteriosis) allows blood to bypass the lungs. This vessel normally closes shortly after birth, but in some dogs it remains open, allowing blood to leak through it and placing a strain on the heart. Affected dogs have a heart murmur, and can be diagnosed definitively with an ultrasound. Surgical correction is necessary to cure the condition. Left untreated, heart failure can result. Patent ductus arteriosis is the most common congenital heart defect in dogs. Evidence is consistent with a polygenic trait that is exhibited once a certain threshold if passed.

## NEURAL DISORDERS

Less common neural disorders with a possible hereditary basis that have been reported in Jack Russell Terriers include:

- **Cerebellar Ataxia:** The cerebellum is part of the brain responsible for the ability to make smooth, coordinated movements. In some dogs, some cells (the Purkinje cells) of the cerebellum degenerate, causing incoordination, most often evidenced by a staggering gait. Signs begin as early as three months of age, and may or may not become progressively worse.

- **Hydrocephalus:** The brain normally has areas filled with cerebrospinal fluid, but in some dogs the fluid is not drained from these areas as it should be, resulting in accumulation of fluid in the brain. Because the skull limits the brain from expansion past a certain point, the pressure builds up, eventually causing brain damage. Even with treatment (which may include diuretic medication or surgical drainage) dogs may have life-long learning deficits. Hydrocephalus may be induced by environmental factors or may be hereditary.

- **Scotty Cramp:** In affected dogs, exercise, excitement, or stress elicits uncontrolled muscle contractions

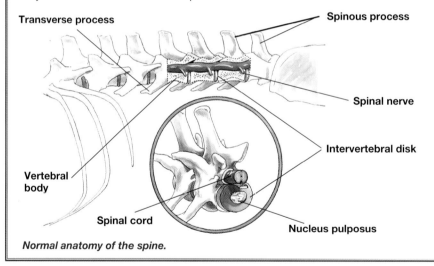

Transverse process

Spinous process

Spinal nerve

Intervertebral disk

Vertebral body

Spinal cord

Nucleus pulposus

*Normal anatomy of the spine.*

## von Willebrand's Disease

Canine von Willebrand's disease (vWD) is a hereditary deficiency in one of the clotting factors that can lead to excessive bleeding. Blood clotting depends not only on a sufficient number of platelets in the blood, but also on a chain of chemical reactions of molecules known as clotting factors. Each successive factor in the chain reaction is identified numerically; in vWD, factor VIII is abnormal or deficient. The degree of deficiency varies between affected

## NEURAL DISORDERS (continued)

(cramping), causing muscle spasms, a stiff gait, and "bunny hopping." Symptoms are usually seen by 18 months of age. In the Scottish Terrier, the breed in which it is best known, it is thought to be caused by a singe recessive allele.

• **Cervical Vertebral Instability:** More commonly referred to as Wobbler's Syndrome, cervical vertebral instability is caused by instability of the intervertebral disks of the neck. Secondary changes can cause compression of the spinal cord, causing not only neck pain, but also loss of coordination of the rear legs, and sometimes paralysis.

• **Congenital Vestibular Disease:** The vestibular sense is responsible for maintaining balance. In some dogs a congenital disorder of the vestibular system manifests itself as early as four months of age. The dog may fall, circle, have a head tilt, and lose its hearing. The eyes may dart back and forth and the dog may be deaf. Although many of the symptoms improve with age, deafness is permanent.

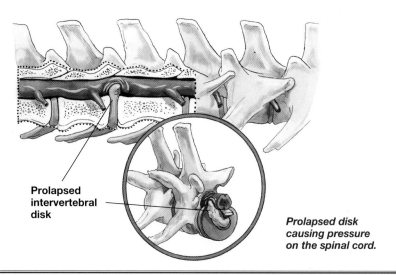

Prolapsed intervertebral disk

*Prolapsed disk causing pressure on the spinal cord.*

individuals because of a somewhat randomized factor in the nature of the mutation that causes it. Dogs with only a slight deficiency will have few symptoms, but those with a greater deficiency may have prolonged or uncontrolled bleeding during surgeries or from cuts, lameness from bleeding into the joints, hematomas (accumulations of blood beneath the skin), nosebleeds, and other abnormal bleeding.

A simple blood test is available, but the results have a great deal of fluctuation. About 10 percent of this variability is from variations in the test itself, but most of the variation is due to variations within the dog's production of von Willebrand factor. This means that a dog with a suspicious test result should be retested several times before concluding it is affected.

A dog that also has hypothyroidism is more likely to have lower von Willebrand factor, so dogs with suspected vWD should be checked for thyroid function. A dog with vWD should be treated with a drug (desmopressin acetate) that increases clotting ability prior to surgery. Although vWD has been reported in JRT's, it does not appear to be a major problem in the breed. It appears to be inherited as an incomplete dominant, so that dogs with one copy of the abnormal gene will have fewer symptoms than dogs with two copies.

*Hello, world!*

# Endocrine

The endocrine system includes several glands that secrete hormones, which are chemicals that travel via the bloodstream to cells and tissues in the body, regulating their function. Endocrine system disorders include diabetes, Cushing's syndrome (see page 190), Addison's disease, and others, but the main endocrine disorder diagnosed in all pure breeds is hypothyroidism.

## Hypothyroidism

The thyroid glands are located near the dog's "Adam's apple" (larynx) in the neck and produce calcitonin, a hormone necessary for normal calcium metabolism, and thyroxine (T4), a hormone that regulates metabolism and is essential for the normal function of many of the body's organs and systems. In some dogs the thyroid gland doesn't make enough hormones, usually because the thyroid gland degenerates from being attacked by the body's own immune system, or for other unknown reasons.

Hypothyroidism is the most commonly seen endocrine problem in purebred dogs. It is diagnosed more often in spayed and neutered dogs. However, many investigators believe hypothyroidism is overdiagnosed. A correct diagnosis entails relating both clinical signs of the disease with laboratory test results indicative of impaired thyroid function.

**Diagnosis:** Clinical signs include hair loss on the flanks, tail, or behind the ears; darkened and thickened skin, sometimes with scaling or seborrhea; weight gain, lethargy, intolerance to cold, slowed heart rate, and infertility, among others. Don't assume your JRT is hypothyroid based only on clinical signs, however.

The simplest test for hypothyroidism is a blood test for baseline serum T4 level. This test, however, is only recommended for identifying dogs with normal thyroid function; it should never be used as the final test to diagnose abnormal thyroid function. Dogs with T4 levels in the higher or even middle part of the normal range are probably not hypothyroid. Dogs with T4 levels in the lower part of the normal range may be in the early stages of hypothyroidism. Dogs with T4 levels below the normal range are suspected of hypothyroidism, but keep in mind that dogs that are sick, have recently undergone anesthesia, or are taking some drugs (including steroids, some nonsteroidal anti-inflammatories, and anticonvulsants), may have a misleadingly low T4 value. Thus, dogs with low T4 values should have additional testing.

More definitive tests include free T4 measured by equilibrium dialysis (fT4ed) and canine thyroid stimulating hormone (cTSH) measurements. In the cTSH stimulation test, T4 levels are measured before and six hours after the dog is given a thyroid stimulating hormone (TSH). A dog with a normally functioning thyroid should respond with a much higher level of T4. These tests entail greater expense, and some veterinarians suggest in cases in which financial factors play a role to instead begin the dog on thyroid supplementation, which is relatively inexpensive, and see if the symptoms resolve. The dog is then weaned from the supplementation and if symptoms return, the dog is diagnosed with probable hypothyroidism. The drawback of this approach is that in the meantime the real reason for the dog's problems may be overlooked, and some dogs are not candidates for supplementation.

**Prognosis:** Treatment for hypothyroidism is with daily medication, and progress monitored with retesting in about two months. It is important to perform the tests about four to six hours after thyroid medication is given in order to measure the peak value.

*With careful testing and responsible breeding, the few problems of the Jack Russell Terrier can remain in check. Meanwhile owners must be on the lookout for signs of and new treatments for these problems—and like all dog owners, make the very best of the far too short time we all have to share with our best friends.*

## Chapter Twelve
# Raising Havoc

Of all the problems the Jack Russell faces, their ongoing population explosion is at the top of the list. If you think you are doing the breed a favor by adding to its numbers, you're not. If you think you're doing your female a favor by letting her experience the pain and danger of birth, you're not. If you think you're going to make money, you're too late. There are many reasons for wanting to breed your Jack Russell Terrier, and some are legitimate, but there are many more reasons not to.

## Too Much of a Good Thing

Jack Russell Terriers are everywhere: in movies, television shows, commercials...and in animal shelters. These great dogs appeal to almost everyone, but living with one is not always for the faint of heart. Some people don't care. They breed their Jack, sell the pups, and wash their hands of them. Do they ever wonder what happens to them? After all, far more Jack puppies are born every year than there are homes for

*Reach for the highest standards.*

them. Some of them die of natural causes, but far more die of unnatural causes. Of these, most are struck by cars. Some are poisoned, shot, or die of neglect. Of the survivors, many are lost or given away (and then given away by their next owners, and so on). Many end up in the dog pound or in rescue. Some go to puppy mills or backyard breeders where they are bred as often as possible until they cease to produce and are dumped or euthanized. Some are tied to a chain or stuck in a pen in the backyard where they will sit in solitary confinement without companionship, activity, or shelter for the next ten or more years. Some are physically abused. Some do find good homes, mostly with people who cared enough to do their homework and find good, responsible breeders. In other words, if you want to attract good homes, you need to be a good breeder. Can you live up to the requirements of a good breeder (page 19)? Do the potential parents of your litter live up to the requirements of a good breeding stock (page 173)? Remember these key points about breeding:

• Unless your JRT has proven herself by earning titles and awards in

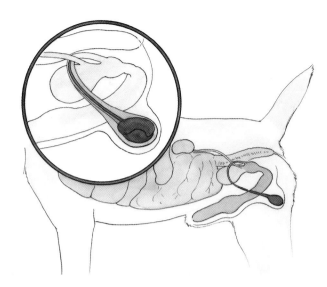

*Male internal organs. The testicles (shown in black) are removed in castration.*

competitions, or by being an outstanding working dog, you may have a difficult time finding good buyers.

• The average litter size for JRT's is six puppies. Breeding so you can keep one pup ignores the fact that five others may not get a good home—or may be ransacking your home for the next 15 years.

• Selling puppies will not come close to reimbursing you for the health clearances, stud fee, prenatal care, whelping complications, Caesarian sections, supplemental feeding, puppy food, vaccinations, advertising, and a staggering investment of time and energy.

• Responsible breeders have spent years researching genetics and the breed, breed only the best specimens that have proven themselves in competition, and screen for hereditary defects in order to obtain superior puppies. Unless you have done the same, you are doing yourself, your dog, the puppies, any buyers, and the breed a great disservice.

---

## ☆ JACK FACT ☆

**For More Information on breeding and genetics:**

Information about
  responsible breeding:           *http://www.dog-play.com/ethics.html*

Canine Diversity Project
  (genetics and health):           *http://www.magma.ca/~kaitlin/diverse.html*

# The Perfect Match

If you're contemplating breeding, it's assumed you've educated yourself about your dog's strengths and weaknesses, have had the appropriate health clearances (page 158), and are familiar with Jack Russell Terrier lines and studs. Choosing a stud will involve several considerations.

## The Stud Dog

Just because your friend has a Jack Russell Terrier doesn't mean that he is marrying potential. If your female is worth breeding, then only the very best male will do as her mate. He should be registered with the same organization (AKC, JRTCA, or another reputable registration body) as your female. He should have earned titles and awards, which not only give an impartial evaluation of him, but will also be helpful in finding good homes. Although no dog is perfect, you need to make sure the two dogs do not share the same faults. Family counts; the male

## TERRIER TECH

### CALCULATING INBREEDING

One way to measure inbreeding is by a technique called path analysis.

**1.** Re-draw your dog's pedigree, but instead of writing it out in the traditional manner, every time the same name appears on *both* the sire's side and the dam's side, write the name only once.

**2.** Draw a path from your dog's sire, back through each of its ancestors to that common ancestor.

**3.** Do the same through your dog's dam. Now you should have a circular path through several generations that goes via both the sire and dam's sides of your dog's pedigree.

**4.** Count the number of steps in the circular pathway from your dog to the common ancestor, and subtract 1 from that number.

**5.** The contribution of each step in the pathway is $(1/2)^n$, where n is the number you got in step 4. For example, $(1/2)^2$ is 0.25, $(1/2)^3$ is 0.125, and $(1/2)^4$ is 0.0625.

**6.** Many dogs will have more than one ancestor common to both sire and dam, so repeat these steps for each common ancestor.

**7.** Add the contributions of each path together, for example, $(1/2)^3 + (1/2)^4 + (1/2)^6$ to obtain the F value, also called the coefficient of inbreeding (COI). In this example F = 0.125 + 0.0625 + 0.015625 = 0.203125, or in plain language, a COI of about 20 percent.

**8.** Note that the COI tends to increase the more generations you include in your analysis, so it's more proper to refer to it as a "COI of an X generation pedigree," where X is the number of generation you included.

**9.** COI also increases if the common ancestor is itself inbred. The adjustment to the calculation is made by multiplying the $(1/2)^n$ result by $(1 + F^a)$, where $F^a$ is the COI of the common ancestor. So, if the common ancestor had a COI of 0.0125, then you would multiply the $(1/2)^n$ value by 1.0125.

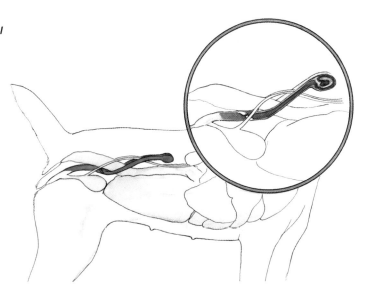

*Female internal organs. The ovary and uterus (shown in black) are removed in spaying.*

should come from a consistently good background. An older (but still fertile) male is preferable, because he has already proven he can live to a healthy old age. He should have at least the same health clearances as your female. If possible, you want to avoid using a very popular sire. Every dog has recessive deleterious genes, even the nicest and most popular studs. It is far better for the health of the breed to maintain genetic diversity by breeding to an equally nice, but less used, stud. Finally, in most cases, you should avoid breeding to a dog closely related to your bitch.

Keep in mind that your choice of stud will be influenced by your plans for registering your pups. If your female is AKC registered, then you will need an AKC registered stud in order for the pups to be AKC registered. If you plan to register the pups

**Spaying and Neutering**

Most veterinarians advocate neutering and spaying dogs that will not be used for breeding. Not only do these procedures negate the chance of accidental litters, but they also do away with the headaches of dealing with a dog in season. In addition, some health benefits are associated with these procedures. Spaying (surgical removal of ovaries and uterus) before the first season drastically reduces the chances of breast or uterine cancer, as well as pyometra. Castration (surgical removal of the testicles) eliminates the chance of testicular cancer. The health benefits are somewhat offset, however, by the slightly lowered metabolism in spayed females, resulting in weight gain unless the dog's diet is monitored carefully. Spayed females also have a higher incidence of urinary incontinence and hypothyroidism.

with the JRTCA, keep in mind that they place restrictions on how closely the sire and dam can be related (see page 34).

The coat types may be crossed, with the rough coat generally dominant to the smooth.

## Genetic Considerations

You should calculate how inbred the resulting puppies would be. The

**_TERRIER-IFIC!_**
One of the top English studs is Ridley Robber of Belmorr, who can be found in the pedigrees of many top winners.

coefficient of inbreeding (COI) refers to the probability that a dog will have identical copies of the same gene that both trace back to the same ancestor. For example, the COI of pups from a sibling to sibling or parent to offspring mating is 25 percent; the COI from a mating of a half-brother to half-sister is 12.5 percent. You can calculate this by hand or with some computer pedigree programs.

Because many deleterious genes are recessive (meaning it takes two

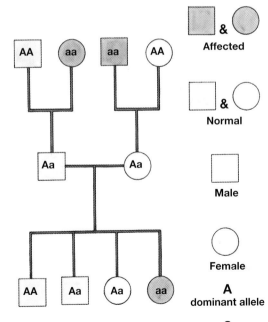

*Inheritance of a recessive trait.*

*Jack pups are into everything.*

identical copies for them to exert their effects on the individual), it's generally a good idea to avoid breedings with high COI's. As a general rule, dogs that are less closely related are more likely to produce healthy and long-lived offspring. Whereas dogs with high COI's are the results of inbreeding, low COI's result from outcrossing. Many geneticists now advocate breeding for the lowest possible COI; however, some compromises will likely need to be made in order to find a dog that otherwise fits your criteria.

# Breeding and Whelping

Arrangements should be made with the stud owner well in advance of the breeding. A written contract should spell out what expenses you'll be responsible for and what will happen if no puppies are born. Count the days from the first sign of estrus carefully, but don't rely on them to determine the right day to breed. If you're shipping your bitch or if there's a lot riding on this breeding, consider monitoring her estrus cycle by means of ovulation timing. Vaginal smears can also give some guidance, but are not nearly as reliable. An experienced stud dog is usually the most reliable indicator of the right time to breed. Most people breed the pair on alternate days for two to three breedings. Dogs ovulate all their eggs within 48 hours, so the idea that runts result from eggs fertilized from later breedings is not valid.

## Pregnancy Determination

Dog gestation is 63 days. Around day 18 to 21 implantation occurs, and during this time some pregnant dogs will appear nauseous and even vomit. A canine pregnancy test (Reprochek) can detect the presence of relaxin, a substance produced by the placenta of a pregnant dog after implantation, typically by day 21 to 25 post-fertilization. Human pregnancy tests don't work because, unlike in humans, even unbred bitches have the same rise in the pregnancy hormones they detect as pregnant ones do. This is why dogs have pseudo-pregnancies; it's normal dog physiology because hormonally they are the same as dogs with real pregnancies.

By about day 35 pregnancy can be determined with ultrasound. Other signs that often develop by then are a mucous discharge from the vagina and enlarged, pinkish nipples. In the last week of pregnancy radiographs can be used to count fetal skeletons. The knowledge of how many puppies to expect can be useful for knowing when the bitch has finished whelping.

The mother-to-be should be kept active throughout most of her pregnancy, but should not be allowed to run and jump too vigorously as she nears her whelping date. She should begin to eat more, gradually switching to puppy food during the latter half of her pregnancy.

## ☆ JACK FACT ☆

**You may have a whelping emergency if:**
• More than 24 hours have passed since her temperature dropped without the onset of contractions.
• More than two hours of intermittent contractions have passed without progressing to hard, forceful contractions.
• More than 30 minutes of strong contractions have passed without producing a puppy.
• More than 15 minutes have passed since part of a puppy protruded through the vulva and the puppy makes no progress.
• Large amounts of blood are passed during whelping.

## ☆ JACK FACT ☆

**Hernias**
Umbilical hernias, in which the opening around the umbilical cord fails to close properly, are a common occurrence in dogs. Most of them are small, and eventually only trap a small pocket of fat. Larger hernias, or ones in which the abdominal contents can become trapped, should be corrected surgically. Although many people believe they come from the umbilical cord being pulled on during whelping, in most cases no such history exists. The hereditary aspects, if any, are not known.

## Whelping

Begin taking the expectant mother's temperature morning and evening every day starting about a week before the due date. When her temperature drops dramatically, to around 98°F (37°C) and stays there, you can anticipate pups within the next 12 hours. She will become increasingly restless and uncomfortable; eventually she will begin to strain with contractions. If a puppy appears stuck, you can use a washcloth and gently pull it downward along with her contractions. Never pull a puppy by a limb, tail, or head, though. You may wish to help the mother clear the pup's face so it can breathe, and you may wish to tie off the umbilical cord. Do this by tying dental floss around the cord about 0.75 inch (around 2 cm) from the pup, and then cutting the cord on the side away from the pup. Make sure that for every pup that comes out, a placenta comes out, too. Allow the dam to eat one placenta if she wants, as they contain important hormones, but they contribute to diarrhea and one is enough.

# Neonatal Care

Monitor the puppies to make sure they are getting milk; pups with cleft palates will have milk bubbling out of their nostrils as they nurse. Use a baby scale to make sure the puppies gain weight every day. Puppies can't regulate their body temperature, and chilling can kill them. Maintain the

---

### ☆ JACK FACT ☆

**Cryptorchidism**

The testicles of male dogs usually migrate from within the abdomen and descend into the scrotum by several weeks of age, although a few dogs may have a much later descent. In some dogs one (unilateral) or both (bilateral) testicles fail to descend and are retained in the body. Unilateral cryptorchids, which are more common, are often referred to as monorchids. Cryptorchidism is found in virtually all breeds of dogs. It is commonly believed to have a genetic component, but the pattern of inheritance has not been discovered.

---

### ☆ JACK FACT ☆

**Docking Puppies' Tails**

If you are going to dock the tails of your puppies, you need to do so between one and three days of age. When docking tails, cut ⅓ off and leave ⅔ on, erring on the side of leaving too much on rather than taking too much off. Keep in mind that some pups are born with naturally short tails; docking ⅓ off of these would result in a much too short tail. Docking is not allowed in several countries, and is not necessary if you don't wish to show your dog. Tails should never be docked as adults except for medical reasons.

temperature in part of the whelping box at about 85°F (29°C) for the first week, 80°F (26°C) for the second week, and 75°F (23.7°C) for the third and fourth weeks. Overheating and dehydration can also have just as devastating effects, so make sure the pups can crawl away from the heat.

Some neonates die for no apparent reason. Probably some of these are victims of canine herpes. Affected pups cry piteously and will not nurse. The herpes virus cannot replicate in high temperatures, and some pups have been saved by placing them in incubators at the first sign of symptoms. If you suspect canine herpes, keep your pups very warm and consult your veterinarian immediately.

The puppies' eyes will begin to open at around 10 days of age, and

the ears at around two weeks. Around this time they will also start attempting to walk. Be sure to give them solid footing—not slippery newspaper!

## Weaning

The dam will begin to wean them at around four to six weeks. Introduce them to pureed puppy food just before they nurse—and be prepared to clean up a major disaster area. You should be checking the dam's mammary glands throughout

*Raising puppies is hard work for everybody.*

**179**

*If you thought one Jack kept you on your toes, you haven't seen anything yet!*

for signs of mastitis, which include pain, bloody discharge, and hard swelling. Home care includes hot compresses and gentle expression of the affected gland, while preventing pups from nursing from it. Call your veterinarian for advice; antibiotics may be necessary.

# Deworming

Ask your veterinarian about the vaccination and deworming regime he or she recommends. Some controversy exists about the traditional series of shots and deworming, so your vet may give you choices and you should be ready to ask questions.

### Intestinal Parasites

Even pups from the most fastidious breeders get worms. This is because some types of larval worms become encysted in the dam's body long before she ever became pregnant; perhaps when she herself was a pup. Here they lie dormant and immune from worming, until hormonal changes caused by her pregnancy activate them, and then they infect her fetuses or her newborns through her milk.

**Ascarids:** The ascarid *Toxocara canis* is found in most pups. Toxocara can be spread to people as well as dogs through infested feces. Infected puppies can also become quite ill, with heavy infestations leading to convulsions or death. Symptoms include a rough coat, potbelly, and wasting muscles. Sometimes adult worms can be seen in vomit or feces. Puppies should be wormed at least twice for Toxocaris, and many protocols advocate more frequent worming.

**Hookworms:** Hookworms are especially prevalent in warm, humid climates. Puppies with heavy infestations have bloody, black, or tarry diarrhea, and can become anemic and die. Adult dogs usually build up an immunity to hookworms, although some dogs have chronic hookworm disease.

**Whipworms:** Whipworms inhabit the large intestine; heavy infestation can cause diarrhea, anemia, and weight loss. Unlike some other types of internal parasites, dogs do not develop an immunity to whipworms. Treatment consists of repeated deworming, often every other month for a year.

**Protazoan intestinal parasites:** Puppies and dogs also suffer from protozoan intestinal parasites, such as coccidia and giardia.

Coccidia are often associated with diarrhea, but many infected dogs show no apparent symptoms. Thus,

---

### ☆ JACK FACT ☆

**Heartworm**

Wherever mosquitoes are present, dogs should be on heartworm prevention. Monthly preventives don't stay in the dog's system for a month, but instead act on a particular stage in the heartworm's development. Giving the drug each month prevents any heartworms from ever maturing. The most common way of checking for heartworms is to check the blood for circulating microfilarae (the immature form of heartworms), but this method may fail to detect the presence of adult heartworms in as many as 20 percent of all tested dogs. More accurate is an "occult" heartworm test, which detects antigens to heartworms in the blood. With either test, the presence of heartworms will not be detectable until nearly seven months after infection. Heartworms are treatable in their early stages, but the treatment is expensive and not without risks (although a less risky treatment has recently become available). If untreated, heartworms can kill your Jack.

coccidia infection in dogs is not well understood at present. A stool sample is needed for diagnosis. Affected dogs respond well to supportive treatment and drugs to do away with the coccidia.

Giardia is found fairly commonly in puppies and dogs. It can cause chronic or intermittent diarrhea, but may also have no symptoms. Giardia can be diagnosed with a stool sample, and is more likely to be found in loose or light-colored stool. Giardia can be treated with drug therapy.

# Vaccinations

Vaccinations save lives. Although some disagreement exists over whether too many vaccinations can have detrimental effects in some dogs, the fact that they are absolutely essential to your dog's well-being is beyond dispute.

Puppy vaccinations are some of the most vital, but most confusing, of all the vaccinations your dog will receive. Puppies receive their dam's immunity from colostrum, the special type of milk the dam produces in the first days of life. This is why it is important that the dam is properly immunized long before breeding, and that her pups are able to nurse from her. The immunity gained from the dam will wear off after several weeks, and then the pup will be susceptible to disease unless you provide immunity through vaccinations. The problem is that there is no way to know exactly when this passive immunity will wear off, and vaccinations given before that time are ineffective. So you must revaccinate over a period of weeks so that your pup will not be unprotected and will receive effective immunity. That's why puppies get a series of shots instead of just one or two.

Vaccinations are available for several diseases. Some vaccinations are mandatory from a legal standpoint, some mandatory from a good sense standpoint, and some optional. Recent studies have implicated repeated vaccinations using combinations of vaccines with some autoimmune problems (see page 151). Some veterinarians thus recommend staggering different types of vaccines, and discourage overvaccination. They also discourage vaccination in any dog that is under stress or not feeling well. Many dogs seem to feel under the weather for a day or so after getting their vaccinations, so don't schedule your appointment the day before boarding, a trip, or a big doggy event.

The common vaccines are:

## Rabies

Rabies is passed mostly through the saliva of carnivores and bats. It is inevitably fatal once symptoms have appeared. Because of its deadly consequences, state laws mandate

*Every life stage is special.*

that all dogs must be vaccinated. The initial rabies vaccination should be given at around three to four months of age, again one year from the first vaccination, and then every three years (although to comply with local law you may have to give a booster every year).

## Distemper

Distemper is seen almost exclusively in unvaccinated puppies. Initial symptoms are upper respiratory problems and fever, followed by vomiting, diarrhea, and neurologic signs. Very young puppies (about six weeks old) usually get a distemper/measles vaccination, because the

*A long life is no accident.*

measles fraction can give temporary immunity even in the presence of maternal antibodies. Subsequent distemper inoculations are given every three to four weeks until the pup is about sixteen weeks old.

## Hepatitis

Infectious canine hepatitis type 1 is most often seen in puppies. It is highly contagious and incurable—even fatal. An adenovirus (called CAV-1) is the causative agent, but vaccination is with CAV-2 (which works just as well but doesn't result in the "blue-eye" reaction that CAV-1 caused when it was used years ago).

## Leptospirosis

Leptospirosis is a bacterial disease, more prevalent in rural areas, that causes serious liver, kidney, and blood abnormalities. Vaccination for "lepto" does not protect against all strains of leptospirosis, and even then only protects for about three to six months. A small percentage of puppies have a transient adverse reaction to the vaccination. Thus, some people prefer not to include lepto in their vaccination regime.

## Parvovirus

"Parvo" is extremely contagious, often fatal, and can remain in the environment for years. Its effects are especially devastating in puppies. Vaccination for parvovirus is often interfered with by maternal antibodies; for this reason three vaccinations by the age of sixteen weeks are recommended, with an optional fourth at around eighteen to twenty weeks.

## Coronavirus

Coronavirus causes extreme diarrhea, in rare cases resulting in death. Younger dogs are most adversely affected. A vaccination is available, but is considered optional currently.

## Tracheobronchitis (Kennel Cough)

Kennel cough is highly contagious. Vaccinations are available, but the problem is that kennel cough can be caused by many different infectious agents. The vaccines protect against the most common ones (CPIV, CAV-2, and bordetella), but not all. Their effects also do not last very long. For these reasons, and because kennel cough is not fatal, some people prefer not to vaccinate for it.

## Lyme Disease

Lyme disease is known to cause severe problems in humans, but its effects in dogs are less clear cut. A vaccination is available but is not universally accepted as necessary. Only dogs living in endemic areas should be considered candidates for Lyme disease vaccination.

## Booster Shots

Several respected veterinary teaching hospitals have recently revised their vaccination protocols to include fewer booster shots. One such protocol suggests giving a three shot series for puppies, each shot containing parvovirus, adenovirus 2 (CAV-2), parainfluenza (CPIV), and distemper, with one rabies vaccination at sixteen weeks.

Following this a booster is given one year later, and then subsequent boosters are given every three years. Other respected epidemiologists disagree and prefer the traditional vaccination schedule. Confer with your veterinarian about current thinking on the matter. One thing is for sure: no matter what their possible side effects, vaccinations are a good thing, and all dogs must be vaccinated for their health as well as the health of others.

# The World Ahead

It's important that the puppies get out to meet people and be socialized in the ways of the world, but at the same time you must be careful about contagious disease. Your pups should be leash trained and crate trained before they go to new homes. They should have spent time away from their littermates. They should have had some car riding experience and met men, women, and children. During all this, they've probably burrowed deep into your heart.

*Now comes the hardest part of breeding a litter: Saying good-bye to the pups you've grown to love, and whose futures you are sealing with your choices about potential buyers. Screen carefully, and don't be afraid to ask prying questions. Your puppies are depending on you.*

*Of course, you could always keep them all...*

## Chapter Thirteen

# The Friend of a Lifetime

With good care and good luck, one day you'll notice your perpetual puppy has finally calmed down, and on closer inspection you may realize her face has silvered and gait has stiffened. Many people feel dogs aren't living as long as they used to, whether from the cumulative effects of inbreeding with a limited gene pool or environmental toxins. No data exist to prove such theories, but in either case it should be noted that many people have unrealistic expectations about life expectancy for their dog, based upon the publicity given to unusually long-lived individuals. All dogs age at different rates, but by ten years of age most Jack Russell Terriers can be considered seniors, although they may still act like juvenile delinquents. Jack Russell Terriers are a fairly long-lived breed, typically reaching twelve to thirteen years of age, and with ages of fifteen to eighteen not rare. However young at heart, at some point your Jack will begin to feel the effects of age, and you will need to know how to best help her cope.

*Jack Russells wear their age well.*

## The Best of Care

Even if your older Jack refuses to act her age, some steps should be taken to ensure that she continues to feel young both in body and soul. However, that doesn't mean she has to go into retirement.

### Behavior

Older dogs tend to like a simpler life, and although they still are up for adventure, that adventure may need to be toned down or abbreviated. Hunting excursions should be made less strenuous.

Long trips can be grueling for an older dog, and boarding in a kennel may be upsetting. Consider getting a house sitter that your dog knows if you want to go on vacation.

Some older dogs become cranky and impatient, especially when dealing with puppies or boisterous children. But don't just excuse behavioral changes, especially if they are sudden. They could be symptoms of pain or disease.

### Exercise

Many JRT owners can't help but have the idea that their dog will never slow down with age. Jack Russells do age well, but staying in a state of denial about your dog's increasing age or decreasing abilities is not doing her any favors. It's important to keep your older dog relatively active, without putting too much stress on her joints. If your dog is sore the next day, you have probably asked too much. Swimming is an excellent low-impact exercise, as long as the water and weather are warm.

While Jacks of any age enjoy a warm, soft bed, it is an absolute necessity for an older Jack. Arthritis is a common cause of intermittent stiffness and lameness, and it can be helped with heat, a soft bed, moderate exercise, and possibly drug therapy. New arthritis medications have made a huge difference in the quality of life for many older dogs, but not every dog can use them. Ask your veterinarian to evaluate your dog.

### Sensory Loss

Older dogs may experience hearing or visual loss. Dogs with hearing loss can learn hand gestures and also respond to vibrations (see page 153).

Dogs with gradual vision loss can cope well as long as they are kept in familiar surroundings, and extra safety precautions are followed. For example, block open stairways or pools, don't move furniture, and place sound or scent beacons throughout the house or yard to help the dog locate specific landmarks. Also lay pathways, such as gravel or block walkways outdoors, and carpet runners indoors. The slight haziness that appears in the older dog's pupils is normal and has minimal effect upon vision, but some dogs, especially those with diabetes, may develop cataracts. These can be seen as almost white through the dog's pupils. The lens can be removed by a veterinary ophthalmologist if the cataract is severe.

### Feeding

Keeping an older dog in ideal weight can be a difficult challenge. Both physical activity and metabolic rates decrease in older animals, so they require fewer calories to maintain the same weight. Excessive weight can place an added burden on the heart and the joints. However, very old dogs often tend to lose weight, which can be equally bad. Your dog needs a little cushion of fat so that she has something to fall back on if she gets sick. Most older dogs do not require a special diet unless they have a particular medical need for it (see page 44). High quality (not quantity) protein is especially important for healthy older dogs.

Older dogs should be fed several small meals instead of one large meal, and should be fed on time. Moistening dry food or feeding canned food can help a dog with dental problems enjoy its meal. Dogs with arthritis, especially affecting the neck, may find it more comfortable to eat elevated food or to eat while lying down.

# Senior Health

The older Jack should have a checkup at least twice a year. Blood tests can detect early stages of treatable diseases. Although older dogs present a somewhat greater anesthesia risk, a complete medical workup before anesthesia can be helpful in evaluating your dog's anesthesia risk.

The immune system may be less effective in older dogs, so that it is increasingly important to shield your dog from infectious disease, chilling, overheating, and any stressful conditions. At the same time, an older dog that is never exposed to other dogs may not need to be vaccinated as often or for as many diseases as a younger dog. This is an area of current controversy, and you should discuss this with your veterinarian.

Vomiting and diarrhea in an old dog can signal many different problems; keep in mind that an older dog cannot tolerate the dehydration that results from continued vomiting or diarrhea and you should not let it continue unchecked.

Like people, dogs lose skin moisture as they age, and though dogs don't have to worry about wrinkles, their skin can become dry and itchy. Regular brushing can help by stimulating oil production. Older dogs tend to have a stronger body odor, but don't just ignore increased odors. They could indicate specific problems, such as periodontal disease, impacted anal sacs, seborrhea, ear infections, or even kidney disease. In

general, any ailment that an older dog has is magnified in severity compared to the same problems in a younger dog.

Periodontal disease is extremely common in older dogs, often the result of years of tooth neglect. The dog may lick her lips constantly, or be reluctant to chew, or even have swelling around the mouth. A thorough tooth cleaning, possibly with more extensive therapeutics is necessary to relieve these dogs' discomfort.

---

## ☆ JACK FACT ☆

**Symptoms and their possible causes in older dogs**

- diarrhea: kidney or liver disease, pancreatitis
- coughing: heart disease, tracheal collapse, lung cancer
- difficulty eating: periodontal disease, oral tumors
- decreased appetite: kidney, liver, or heart disease, pancreatitis, cancer
- increased appetite: diabetes, Cushing's syndrome
- weight loss: heart, liver or kidney disease, diabetes, cancer
- abdominal distention: heart or kidney disease, Cushing's syndrome, tumor
- increased urination: diabetes, kidney or liver disease, cystitis, Cushing's syndrome
- limping: arthritis, hip or elbow dysplasia, degenerative myelopathy
- nasal discharge: tumor, periodontal disease

*Cushing's syndrome (hyperadrenocorticism)* is seen mostly in older dogs, and is characterized by increased drinking and urination, potbellied appearance, symmetrical hair loss on the body, darkened skin, and susceptibility to infections. Diagnosis is with a blood test. Treatment is with drug therapy.

Dogs suffer from many of the same diseases of old age that humans do. Cancer accounts for almost half of all deaths in dogs over ten years of age. Some signs of cancer are abnormal swellings that don't go away or that continue to grow, loss of appetite or difficulty eating or swallowing, weight loss, persistent lameness, bleeding, or difficulty breathing, urinating, or defecating. Most of these symptoms could also be associated with other disorders, so that only a veterinary examination can determine the real problem.

*Always hold close the memories you made with your Jack Russell, a true partner in life and adventure.*

If you are lucky enough to have a Jack senior, you still must accept that your time together is all the more precious and ultimately will end. Heart disease, kidney failure, and cancer eventually claim most of these seniors. Early detection can help delay their effects, but unfortunately, can seldom prevent them ultimately.

# When You've Done Everything

Perhaps it is their cherublike air of eternal youth; perhaps it is the never-fading look of sheer delight in thinking up yet another novel piece of mischief; perhaps it is just that we love them so—but facing the inevitable truth that one day even the most loved and well-cared-for Jack must eventually leave is almost beyond comprehension. It's hard to believe that you will have to say good-bye to someone who has been such a companion, family member, and partner in adventure. Yet that time will come.

### Grief

Denial is the first stage of grief, and the first reaction dog owners usually have to the news that their dog has a terminal illness. It's a natural reaction that protects us from the emotional impact of the painful truth. It also goads many people into seeking a second opinion and exploring every possibility for curing their friend. Often, as it becomes clear that nothing can help, the next stage of grief is anger—anger that dogs live so short a time, anger that the treatments for humans are not available to dogs, and even anger at those who have older dogs. The third stage of grief is depression, when the truth is accepted and the futility of fighting acknowledged. Depression can begin well before actually losing a dog, and last well after. It can involve such a feeling of helplessness and defeat that a person may not even try some reasonable therapies for their dog. Although depression is natural, protracted depression can be extremely damaging. As painful as grief is, it is hard to let go of, perhaps because to do so is to finally say good-bye. At that point, the last stage of grief is acceptance. Accepting the loss of a loved one doesn't mean you don't care; it just means that you realize that you have to do so in order to continue living and loving again. In deciding what is best for you and your dog, and in getting through this terribly difficult part of your life, consider how your stage of grieving may be affecting your decisions.

## Euthanasia

Many terminal illnesses make your dog feel very ill, and there comes a point where your desire to keep your friend with you as long as possible may not be the kindest thing for either of you. If your dog consistently declines to eat, this is usually a sign that he doesn't feel well, and a signal that you must begin to face the

> ☆ **JACK FACT** ☆
>
> Rainbow Bridge Tribute Page dealing with the loss of a pet *http://rainbowbridge.tierranet. com/bridge.htm*

prospect of doing what is best for your beloved friend.

Euthanasia is a difficult and personal decision that no one wants to make. Consider if your dog has a reasonable chance of getting better, and how your dog seems to feel. Ask yourself if your dog is getting pleasure out of life, and if he enjoys most of his days. Financial considerations can be a factor if it means going into debt in exchange for just a little while longer. Your emotional state must also be considered. For every person the ultimate point is different. Most people probably put off doing something for longer than is really the kindest thing because they don't want to act in haste and be haunted by thoughts that just maybe it was a temporary setback. And of course, they put it off because they can't stand the thought.

We all wish that if our dog has to go, he would fall asleep and never wake up. This, unfortunately, seldom happens. Even when it does, you are left with the regret that you never got to say good-bye. The closest you can come to this is with euthanasia. Euthanasia is painless and involves giving an overdose of an anesthetic. Essentially the dog will fall asleep and die almost instantly. In a very sick dog, because the circulation may be compromised, this may take slightly longer, but the dog is not conscious.

If you do decide that euthanasia is the kindest farewell gesture for your beloved friend, discuss with your veterinarian beforehand what will happen. You may ask about giving your dog a tranquilizer beforehand, or having the doctor meet you at home. Although it won't be easy, try to remain with your dog so that its last moments will be filled with your love. Try to recall the wonderful times you have shared and realize that however painful losing such a once-in-a-lifetime friend is, it is better than never having had such a partner at all.

# Eternal in Your Heart

Partnership with a pet can be one of the closest and most stable relationships in many people's lives. Many people who regarded their Jack Russell Terrier as a true friend and member of the family nonetheless feel embarrassed at the grief they feel at its loss. Unfortunately, the support from friends that comes with human loss is too often absent with pet loss. Some people who have never shared such a bond with a dog don't understand, and others who do may still not be able to express their feelings of condolences as readily as they would with human loss. Many people share and understand your feelings, however, and pet bereavement counselors are available at many veterinary schools.

After losing such a cherished friend, many people say they will never expose themselves to that kind of pain by loving another dog. Some also see giving their love to another dog as being unfaithful to the first. No dog will ever take the place of your departed dog, and the love you have for it will not be lessened by loving another. If you had so much to give and share with one dog, the only worse loss would be never sharing it again.

The loss of a companion may mark the end of an era for you, a time when you and your friend grew up or grew old together. But a new adventure is on the horizon—share it with a special friend with a cold nose and a warm heart.

# Jackpot of Information

## Organizations

The Jack Russell Terrier Club of
America, Inc.
P.O. Box 4527
Lutherville, MD 21094-4527
(410) 561-3655
*http://www.terrier.com/index.php3*

The Jack Russell Terrier Association
of America
Maria Sacco, Secretary
P.O. Box 3223
Alexandria, VA 22302
e-mail: *jrtaa@usa.net*
(203) 379-3282
*http://www.jrtaa.org/*

The Jack Russell Terrier Club of
Canada
Yvonne Downey
242 Henrietta Street
Fort Erie, Ontario
Canada, L2A 2K7
(905) 871-8691

The Jack Russell Terrier Club of
Great Britain
Chairperson: Greg Mousley
Aston Heath Farm
Sudbury, Derbyshire
England DEGS88

English Jack Russell Terrier Club
Alliance
3 Columbia 61
Magnolia, AR 71753
e-mail: *EJRTCA@aol.com*
*http://www.ejrtca.com/*

The American Working Terrier
Association
Patricia Adams Lent
503 NC 55 West
Mt. Olive, NC 28465
*http://www.dirt-dog.com/awta/
index.shtml*

American Kennel Club (AKC)
5580 Centerview Drive
Raleigh, NC 27606-3390
(919) 233-9767
e-mail: *info@akc.org*
*http://www.akc.org/*

Canadian Kennel Club
89 Skyway Avenue, Suite 100
Etobicoke, Ontario
Canada, M9W 6R4
(800) 250-8040
e-mail: *information@ckc.ca*
*http://www.ckc.ca/*

United Kennel Club (UKC)
100 East Kilgore Road
Kalamazoo, MI 49001-5593
(616) 343-9020
http://www.ukcdogs.com/

American Dog Owner's Association
1654 Columbia Turnpike
Castleton, NY 12033
(518) 477-8469
e-mail: adoa@global2000.net

American Temperament Testing
   Society
P.O. Box 397
Fenton, MO 63026
(314) 225-5346
http://www.atts.org/

Canine Eye Registration Foundation
   (CERF)
1248 Lynn Hall, Purdue University
West Lafayette, IN 47907
(765) 494-8179
http://www.vet.purdue.edu:80/
   ~yshen/cerf.html

Orthopedic Foundation for Animals
2300 E. Nifong Blvd.
Columbia, MO 65201
(573) 442-0418
e-mail: ofa@offa.org
http://www.offa.org/

Home Again Microchip Service
1-800-LONELY-ONE

Therapy Dogs International
88 Bartley Road
Flanders, NJ 07836
(973) 252-9800
e-mail: tdi@gti.net
http://www.tdi-dog.org/

Canine Performance Events (CPE)
P.O. Box 445
Walled Lake, MI 48390
e-mail: cpe-agility@juno.com

Agility Association of Canada (AAC)
RR#2
Lucan, Ontario
Canada, N0N 2J0
(519) 657-7636

United States Dog Agility Association
   (USDAA)
P.O. Box 850995
Richardson, TX 75085-0955
(972) 231-9700
e-mail: info@usdaa.com
http://www.usdaa.com/

## Rescue

JRTCA Russell Rescue
Catherine Romaine Brown
P.O. Box 24
Geneseo, NY 14454-9731
(716) 226-2826
e-mail: brownacorn@aol.com
http://www.terrier.com/rescue/
   contacts.php3

JRTAA Rescue
Karyn Collins
(860) 445-1390
e-mail: Karyn4Dave@aol.com

## Periodicals

*True Grit*
Official publication of the JRTCA

*JRTAA Newsletter*
Official publication of the JRTAA

*Down to Earth*
Official publication of the AWTA

*AKC Gazette*
(covers general aspects of all breeds)
AKC Order Desk
5580 Centerview Drive
Raleigh, NC 27606-3390
(919) 233-9767
e-mail: *orderdesk@akc.org*
*http://www.akc.org/insideAKC/
    resources/subs.cfm*

*Dog Fancy*
P.O. Box 53264
Boulder, CO 80322-3264
(303) 666-8504

*Dog World*
500 N. Dearborn, Suite 1100
Chicago, IL 60610
(312) 396-0600
e-mail: *Info@dogworldmag.com*
*http://www.dogworldmag.com/*

*Clean Run* (covers agility)
35 Walnut Street
Turners Falls, MA 01376
(800) 311-6503; fax (413) 863-8303
email: *info@cleanrun.com*
*http://www.cleanrun.com/*

Dog World Magazine
P.O. Box 56240
Boulder, CO 80322-6240
(800) 361-8506
http://www.dogworldmag.com/

Front and Finish (covers obedience)
H & S Publications, Inc.
P.O. Box 333
Galesburg, IL 61402-0333
e-mail: frntfnsh@galesburg.net
http://www.frontfinish.com/

## Books

Atter, Sheila. *Jack Russell Terriers Today.* Gloucestershire, Great Britain: Ringpress Books, Ltd., 1995.

Britt-Hay, Deborah. *The Complete Idiot's Guide to Owning, Raising, and Training a Jack Russell Terrier.* New York, NY: Howell Book House, 1999.

Brown, Catherine Romaine. *The Jack Russell Terrier: Courageous Companion.* New York, NY: Howell Book House, 1999.

Chapman, Eddie. *The Working Jack Russell Terrier.* Dorchester, Great Britain: Henry King at the Dorset Press, 1985.

Coile, D. Caroline. *Encyclopedia of Dog Breeds.* Hauppauge, NY: Barron's Educational Series, Inc., 1998.

———. *Show Me! A Dog Showing Primer.* Hauppauge, NY: Barron's Educational Series, Inc., 1997.

———. *Jack Russell Terriers: A Complete Pet Owner's Manual.* Hauppauge, NY: Barron's Educational Series, Inc., 2000.

Frier-Murza, Jo Ann. *Earthdog Ins & Outs.* Centreville, AL: OTR Publications, 1999.

Jackson, Jean and Frank. *The Making of the Parson Jack Russell Terrier.* Dover, NH: The Boydell Press, 1986.

———. *Parson Jack Russell Terriers: An Owner's Companion.* Great Britain: The Crowood Press, 1991.

———. *Parson Jack Russell Terriers: An Owner's Companion.* Great Britain: The Crowood Press, 1990.

———. *The Parson and Jack Russell Terriers.* London: Popular Dogs Publishing Co, Ltd., 1991.

James, Ken. *Working Jack Russell Terriers.* Bedford, PA: Hunter House Press, 1995.

Lent, Patricia. *Sport With Terriers.* Rome, NY: Arner Publications, 1973.

Massey, Marilyn. *Above and Below Ground: The Jack Russell Terrier in North America.* Millwood, VA: Woodluck Publications, 1985.

Plummer, D. Brian. *The Complete Jack Russell Terrier.* New York, NY: Howell Book House, 1980.

Strom, Mary. *The Ultimate Jack Russell Terrier.* New York, NY: Howell Book House, 1999.

## Web Addresses

| | |
|---|---|
| Animal CPR | *http://members.aol.com/henryhbk/acpr.html* |
| Plank Road JRT Site | *http://plank-road.com/* |
| Dirt Dog Web Page | *http://www.Dirt-Dog.com/index.shtml* |
| Parson Russell Terrier Page (UK) | *http://dialspace.dial.pipex.com/town/square/ gm72/index.htm* |
| Earthdog and Working Terrier Message Board | *http://www.insidetheweb.com/mbs.cgi/mb800771* |
| Jack Russell Photo Gallery | *http://www.geocities.com/Heartland/Ridge/2259/ 100.html* |
| AKC Jack Russell Terrier Information | *http://www.akc.org/breeds/recbreeds/jrt.cfm* |
| Jack Russells Online | *http://www.jackrussells.com/cgi-local/shop.pl/ page=list.html* |
| Earthdog and Squirrel Dog Hunting Homepage | *http://www.k9web.com/dog-faqs/activities/ edsdhp.html* |
| The Dog Agility Page | *http://www.dogpatch.org/agility/* |
| The Dog Obedience and Training Page | *http://www.dogpatch.org/obed/* |
| Dr. P's Dog Training Links | *http://www.uwsp.edu/acad/psych/dog/dog.htm* |
| Infodog Dog Show Site | *http://www.infodog.com/main.htm* |
| National Animal Poison Control Center (800) 548-2423 | *http://www.napcc.aspca.org/* |
| Operant Conditioning in Dog Training | *http://mmg2.im.med.umich.edu/~kleung/ training.html* |
| Rainbow Bridge Tribute Page (deals with the loss of a pet) | *http://rainbowbridge.tierranet.com/bridge.htm* |
| Rescue Information Center | *http://labrynth.simplenet.com/ric/* |
| Steppin' Up-Date Obedience Site | *http://www.dogpro.com/terriarnold/newsletter/ Newsletter1.htm* |
| Take a BowWow Training Site | *http://www.takeabowwow.com/* |
| The Tracking Page | *http://personal.cfw.com/~dtratnac/* |
| AKC Earthdog Clubs | *http://www.akc.org/dic/clubs/other/earthcb.cfm* |

# Index

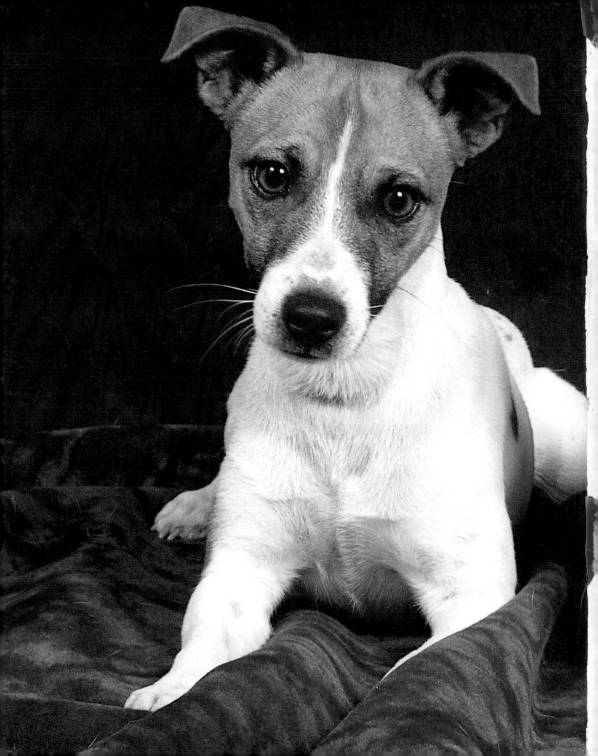